Never Give Up!

# Infinite Persistence Life Book

by GORDON WEINBERGER

Published by Infinite Persistence Publications
2541 Ashland Road
Mansfield, OH 44905


ISBN: 0-9772960-0-8
Library of Congress Control Number: 2005932882
Printed in the United States of America

This publication is designed to provide information and guidance with regard to the subject matter covered. It is sold with the understanding that the publisher and authors are not engaged in rendering legal, medical, accounting, or other professional advice. If legal, medical, or other expert assistance is required, the services of a competent, licensed professional person should be sought.

Cover Photo: Les Carron

Cover Design: jodesign

Research and Writing: Melinda Kaitcer, Diane Legendre, Alyssa Wyman

Editing: Melinda Kaitcer, Kathy Walker

Copy Editing: Jill Scott, Kathy Walker

Endless Support: Cindy, Emily, Jack, Sam

**Infinite Persistence**™ PUBLICATIONS
by Gordon Weinberger

TO SHUGS, FOR ALWAYS BEING THERE.

— G.W.

# Table of Contents

# Introduction

In a conference room high above Atlanta, Georgia, there I was, signing the documents that would complete the sale of my Gordon's Pies brand to Mrs. Smith's Bakeries. It was an unbelievable day — and one that was long in the making. What had begun as a lark — a Saturday morning baking spree with my new wife, Cindy, and my great-grandmother's pie recipe — had gone from novelty to small business to big business to near bankruptcy to rebuilding to branding to marketing strategies many would label as crazy. But through it all I stuck by the words I said out loud in that spare bedroom where my business began. I would **never give up, no matter what**; and I would **sell my company to Mrs. Smith's Bakeries in seven years**. And that's just what I did. I did not give up, even when everyone thought I should, and I signed the Letter of Intent to sell my company to Mrs. Smith's six years and ten months from the day I started my business.

*After winning two pie-baking contests, Gordon Weinberger
decided to open an apple pie bakery in New Hampshire.*

Do you have a dream that would create success
beyond your wildest imaginings? Well, you and I are
a lot alike. I, too, had a dream, and I saw that dream
through to reality, but not without plenty of hard
work and determination.

During the time I was building Gordon's Pies, I didn't
know how to define this dogged determination; I just
knew that I would not quit until I had reached my goals.

After I sold Gordon's Pies to Mrs. Smith's, I took
three years off to reconnect with my family and
myself, and to try to wrap my mind around all that

had happened. During that time, I had a huge epiphany that helped me define this driving concept of "*never give up, no matter what*" as something I began to call *Infinite Persistence*. I also knew without a doubt that I was supposed to share my experience — and this new insight it had brought to me in a very surprising way — with the world.

Infinite Persistence brought me to success beyond my wildest dreams — what a ride it was! And it can do the same for you.

# How to Use This Book

In the *Infinite Persistence Life Book*, I am going to share several important things with you. First, through my own experiences, I will show by example how Infinite Persistence can fill your life with your wildest dreams achieved. Then I will show you how, with continuous focus on your strengths and an idea you believe in, Infinite Persistence is the secret ingredient that makes it all happen — faster and easier than you ever could have imagined.

All that being said, this doesn't mean it is necessarily going to be easy. In the pursuit of my own dream, I made and lost and made millions of dollars. I put myself in all kinds of jeopardy countless times because I didn't understand the true nature of the kind of success Infinite Persistence brings into your life once you decide to embrace it. The good news for you is that you don't have to make the mistakes and endure the hard knocks I did in order to activate this powerful principle in your life. All you have to do is read this book, learn from my experiences, search your own heart, and put the laws of the Universe to work on *your* dreams.

This book is a little different from other materials you may read about creating the life of your dreams. In weaving the principles of Infinite Persistence through my own story and the discoveries that sprang from it, I'll not only tell you the story of Gordon's Pies as it occurred, but I'll also show you where, if I had been aware, the laws of Infinite Persistence came into play — and how, if I had but understood them, they could have guided me on a path that was much more fun and less harrowing.

This is a book to be read and reread. Skip, scan, read, and reread the parts that catch your attention. There's an old saying that the teacher appears when the pupil is ready — and that's the way it will work for you as you move through this book. Some of these words, in one reading, may mean nothing. Then, a few miles down the road, the same words will provide extraordinary insights. At different points of your own journey, changes in your situation will create new layers of understanding. And as you begin working with these simple concepts, you will peel back these layers, like the layers of an onion, to arrive at a few simple, powerful truths that have guided entire civilizations since the beginning of time.

The lessons and principles that my experiences taught me to recognize as Infinite Persistence I call *Slice of the Pi(e)*, and they are woven throughout my story as they naturally occurred. As my experiences unfolded, the model I now call Infinite Persistence also revealed some specific business strategies, which I have dubbed *Seeds of Success*, sown like so many apple seeds throughout my journey. And finally, there are *Core Values* – the things I have learned, many of them the hard way, about living a life of joy and fulfillment beyond monetary success. When you live your life and create a business in alignment with your core values, the successes you achieve will be as sweet, real, and satisfying as hot apple pie.

CHAPTER 1

# Discovering the Power of Pi

$$\pi$$

My concept of Infinite Persistence was born one night in March of 2005. It had been nearly three years since I had sold my company to Mrs. Smith's, and I was watching TV with my six-year-old son, Sam, and there it was. A character on a *Jimmy Neutron* cartoon said, "So what *is* the meaning of pi?" And the word, pi, was boldly imprinted across the screen.

I'm still not sure why, but that image ignited my imagination. My mind raced through the possibilities, and I ran for the computer in my office. Behind me, I heard Sam ask where I was going as I left the room, but I was too focused to answer. Once in my office, I first did a Google search for pi and found an entry that said, "pi = 3.14159." It went on to explain, "Pi has been a part of human culture and the educated imagination for more than twenty-five hundred years ...." The list of entries went on and on — it seemed, well, infinite.

Next, I began to write words related to my search all over the white board in my office. I manically scribbled every connection that came to mind related to pi, the mathematical equations of circles, the underlying, unseen order of the Universe, and the deeper implications of the importance of the circular shape itself. Exhausted, I sat back and stared at the words I had written. The large board was full, edge to edge, but then, almost magically, two words seemed to lift themselves above the rest, drawing themselves into sharp focus while the others blended into the background. Almost floating into the air in front of my eyes were two words: Infinite Persistence.

Somehow I knew that I was on my way again. Establishing Gordon's Pies ten years earlier had been an amazing journey, but now an even more intriguing journey was revealing itself. What Infinite Persistence meant, I had no idea, but my instincts told me without question that this new challenge floating there before my eyes was a huge and undeniable opportunity. Those two words were the tip of the proverbial iceberg, and my gut instinct told me that this concept was something important that I must share with the world. All that I had been through in my ten years in the pie business suddenly made more sense. These experiences were the precursors, the groundwork being laid in me for this new journey. Sharing with others the powerful principle I've come to know as Infinite Persistence (IP) is my new quest — and with it comes my intent to help others learn from my road to success the concepts that can reshape their their lives.

# CHAPTER 2

# So What *IS* the True Meaning of Pi?

In the days and weeks that followed my Jimmy Neutron epiphany, I explored further the concept of pi. The ironic humor of this project, dropped by the Universe into my unsuspecting lap, was not lost on me. Here I was, Gordon, King of Pie, playing with pi, one of the most fundamental concepts of mathematics, to create a life model based on what I had learned in the business of, well, selling *pie*.

To create a model from that moment of inspiration, I first had to relate the term pi — the ratio of a circle's circumference to its diameter — to telling people how they can tap into the infinite power of the never-ending connectedness of the Big Circle — the Universe — and everything and everyone in it. Once we understand that we can have the power of the Universe at our fingertips, we can achieve just about anything we choose to do.

As I explored all the possible implications of what

something called Infinite Persistence could mean, a torrent of other terms flooded my brain. I went back to my office's white board and wrote them: infinity … infinite potential … infinite productivity … and so on. The possibilities created by embracing the idea of Infinite Persistence — the power and magic behind the words "*never give up, no matter what*" — were revealing themselves to me, one by one. Then, somewhere in this process of discovery, the larger truth dawned on me: **When we understand and harness the power of the mathematical connectedness of a circle — the infinity of pi — we create infinite possibilities in our lives.**

## Bringing Pi Back Down to Earth

While all this pi-in-the-sky thinking had my brain humming, I was yet to discover what it was that I was supposed to do with this information. What exactly was I supposed to tell others about it — and how could I communicate these important, but mind-boggling, concepts in a way that would make any sense to the average entrepreneur?

In true circular fashion, I then went back to the beginning — the circle. When we think of a circle, there is no end. If we apply the infinite structure of the circle to our desire for success, we can believe, without fear, that we can go as far as we need to go, for as long as necessary, to become who we were meant to become and do what we were meant to do — and achieve at far higher levels than we ever expected.

Taking this imagery even further, mathematicians will tell you that the very structure of a circle includes an infinite number of *corners*. As we adopt the Infinite Persistence model, we may face many obstacles that can be seen as "corners," turning points, or challenges. And with Infinite Persistence, these obstacles all circle back to become opportunities.

What finally drove it all home for me was the realization that everything we share and everything we seek to achieve will come back to us full circle if we allow it. By expressing our desires, sharing our dreams, and making specific steps toward achieving them, we can accomplish more than we can ever imagine. This powerful circle can have a profound effect on our lives and, ultimately, the entire world.

# A Brief History of Pi

The mathematical equation of pi and the unseen laws of the Universe it sets into motion have been used as a model since ancient times. People around the world have been unknowingly guided by the power behind this mathematical equation, and they have used it in every form imaginable, from literary works ("The Raven" by Edgar Allen Poe encodes the 740 digits of pi within its content) to the construction of the Great Pyramids of Egypt.

With a history that dates back to the ancient Babylonians, pi has been said to be the only relic of ancient mathematics that still interests the modern mathematical world. In these earliest expressions of Infinite Persistence, civilizations were able to achieve their goals and dreams — and create structures which, even today, cannot be completely explained.

Even though the ancients were the first to discover the formula known as pi, the first person to ever use the Greek letter to describe it was William Jones in the year 1706. It was only after Jones used it as an abbreviation for the periphery of a circle that the Greek letter became pi's standard mathematical notation. As I studied the history of pi, I realized that, likewise, for those of us who choose to live a life of persistence, going the distance, and pursuing our passions — "never giving up, no matter what" — "IP" can become *our* standard notation. And just as the formula pi has created passion in people since early times to explore its depths and beyond, realization of our own IP potential creates passion to pursue our wildest dreams and desires.

## A Driving Force

As pi rules the unseen world of mathematics, Infinite Persistence drives us by creating desire in every area of our lives. Our bodies, minds, and hearts are affected by how we persist within the world around us.

Infinite Persistence is what drives our sense of hope, faith, and love. It affects our relationships as we move through the seasons of life, and it determines whether we choose to work through our struggles and disappointments to find the triumphs — or run away in disappointment and fear.

If we choose to persist and move ahead, each moment of success contributes to a momentum that will become larger than any life you ever could have imagined! Visualize a dancer moving fluidly from one stance to another, from one position to another, circling around and around to face the audience anew with each revolution. Infinite Persistence is the catalyst that creates the movement and the beauty in one's life. Your vision will begin each journey, but Infinite Persistence will bring you again and again to a place of triumph. These infinite circles will change and renew your life, even as the circular rotation of the spherical earth allows life to flourish in a dance of continuing cycles.

Carrying this rhythmic analogy even further into the world of music, Infinite Persistence is at the core of the songs that lighten our moods and the tunes that relax us. If composers didn't persist, the infinite beauty of their innate talents would be lost. Yet with Infinite Persistence, they build upon and explore these talents, revealing them again and again in the music that affects us on many different concentric levels.

## Life Is But a Dream

The dreams of any human being who chooses to infinitely persist affect every person he or she comes into contact with — and that effect can be life-changing for everyone involved. Have you ever met someone and in just one moment or in one conversation, your life changed forever? In that one moment, your life's course took a quick turn in a new direction, on a route that can never rejoin your previous path. When you become infinitely persistent, not only do you draw these experiences and people into your life, but in true circular fashion, you become that person for others.

The dreams we have — and the people who come into our life to help bring these dreams to fruition — are all products of the reality we construct from an infinite sea of possibilities. It is when we consciously choose a dream from that sea of infinite possibilities that our reality emerges. This reality includes the people, the opportunities, the timing, and the events that bring the reality you have chosen to life.

Creating our own reality with our thoughts and decisions is indeed tapping into the power of the Universe — and harnessing this power by conscious choice is what makes dreams come true. This infinite circle of creating and responding is exactly what the mathematicians were alluding to when they first began to understand the power of pi. It explained to them how individuals, groups, and even entire civilizations were able to accomplish great, unexplainable things, just by persisting until their wildest dreams became a new reality.

# It's a Matter of Choice — And It's All Yours

Choosing to never give up, no matter what, means creating a reality of success for yourself that draws from the power of the Universe that is, indeed, always available to you. It's simply a matter of realizing that fact and choosing it as your reality. It truly is that simple, despite what we may be conditioned to believe. Exploring these ideas and watching them work as I reached the extremely high goals I had constructed for myself in the pie business became the basis for this lesson that I suddenly knew I must share with others.

Pi and Infinite Persistence are but facets of the mathematical equation of success — one that inspires, enlightens, and demands to be explored.

Is this unseen power to choose our own reality a fleeting, capricious thing? A fluke? Dumb luck? There are those who may say so. But the power of pi and its reflection, IP, is oblivious to our acceptance. Regardless of whether we believe in it, it simply is.

And once we make the conscious choice to embrace this power to choose our own reality, doors begin opening and dreams start coming true. The more you practice choosing your reality and the more you see the results this shift in your thinking brings into your life, the more you create a deeper understanding that this power is indeed possible — and real.

But don't just take my word for it. Try it for yourself. Start with the little stuff. Decide what you want a particular reality to look like, feel like, be like in your life. Focus on it as if it has already happened. Scientists tell us that the brain cannot distinguish between what the eyes see and what it remembers. Hold that reality in your mind and let it resonate in the core of your being. Watch it unfold.

The next thing you know, the people you need to meet will show up; the opportunities you're seeking will appear; doors will open; phones will ring; and the pieces of your new reality will begin to float almost effortlessly into place.

Did I say effortlessly? As you will see from my story, having the pieces to your puzzle of success appear in your life is the easy part. You still have to show up and put your own sweat into it to make it happen. The seeming magic of Infinite Persistence begins in the mind, but carrying out the physical realities of your dreams still requires your own dedicated, hard work. So don't just sit there — choose your reality, watch the opportunities appear, and get after it!

# CHAPTER 3

# Some Famous Words on the Subject

Renowned humanitarian Horatio Alger once said that success is all about "**luck, pluck and virtue.**" He believed that if you had these three things, you could go all the way and achieve your dream. Connecting with the right people as we travel through life, being confident in ourselves and in our beliefs — without fear — and being honest and trustworthy all build the reality dreams are made of. The Infinite Persistence model is but an extension of Alger's philosophy, adding to it some concepts concerning attitude and balance, and strategies for finding the pathways to your dreams.

"**At first, a task looks difficult, then it is impossible, then it is done**" were the insightful words of J. Hudson Taylor, an English missionary to China in the 1800s. Taylor clearly knew about Infinite Persistence. Even as a child, he knew he could choose his reality, and there was never any doubt in his mind that, eventually, if he persisted, the "task" would be done. His path was a difficult one, but he knew with great certainty what he wanted to do with his life. He accomplished his dream by infinitely persisting — and surpassing the many challenges and hardships along the way — to create the reality he had chosen. The infinite power of the Universe opens the doors to our dreams. But it is up to us to supply the persistence in getting through those doors, despite whatever obstacles or challenges fall into our path. Persisting toward your dream will affect your entire life — and everyone in it — as you focus on the end result.

To achieve your dream, you will have to be enduring, strong, and responsible — and willing to learn from the challenges your journey will bring. Know that the hurdles are part of the process, and that when you meet them head on, they will most likely become your best teachers, and often herald the turning points that lead to your ultimate success. Without the hurdles commonly referred to as "the school of hard knocks," there are no turning points. You must remember to *just keep moving forward* — beyond the hurdles — and onward to the successes.

Embracing this understanding that hurdles are essential elements on the road to our achievement diminishes their power to discourage us. Without them, we would lose the opportunity to learn what we need to know.

These twin concepts — *never give up, no matter what,* and allowing the turning points to propel you to success — are the keys to achieving the reality your mind has created. This awareness must remain foremost in your thoughts every single day. Live each day in the power of these key concepts and remind yourself, when you snag your toe on a hurdle and go crashing to the ground, that *not* getting what you *think* you want may be the very thing that makes the difference in reaching your goal.

## Make Friends With Change

Life is a constantly changing reality, and you must learn to see change as a blessing, rather than a threat. As you attain the smaller goals that lead to the achievement of your dream, it is important to understand the nature of the changes that affect your life. Then, as you learn to anticipate and accept these changes, you can eliminate their power to distract you or hold you back.

**"The universe is change; our life is what our thoughts make it."**

*— Marcus Aurelius*

Even the earliest philosophers knew the fundamental truths about change and the power of our thoughts — long before we started rediscovering it and then trying to make sense of these timeless, infinite concepts in modern, concrete terms. Often, we are conditioned to believe that we have no control over reality. But on the contrary, since the beginning of time those who understood the power of the infinite — of Infinite Persistence, if you will — knew the corresponding truth: what happens within us creates what happens outside us. To try to explain this in concrete terms is stepping down a rabbit hole of supposition that has set a timeless and tumultuous collision course for mathematicians, scientists, and theologians worldwide. But to acknowledge it, live it, and accept its power over our individual lives, our realities, and the achievement of our cherished goals is a matter of acceptance and choice. It really is as simple as pie. You don't have to understand it — you just have to, in the immortal words of the fictitious St. Nike, "Just Do It."

# CHAPTER 4

# How to Become Infinitely Persistent

To apply the Infinite Persistence model to your life, the first thing you have to do is think big. Now think bigger. Imagine, as we described in the previous sections, what you would do if you could envision successful reality in your mind's eye. Now plant yourself there in your imagination. I keep the following saying in a prominent place in my office: "What would you attempt to do if you knew you could not fail?" I like to turn this question inside out to put it into action: "Behave as if you cannot fail and choose your actions as if you were unafraid of falling short." It is the only way you will succeed.

My decision to employ Infinite Persistence — which at the time was just a loose, nebulous concept — to the pie business I was planning to start became real to me on that first day of official business in 1994, when I first said out loud, *"I will never give up, no matter what."*

Once that vow was squarely established at the core of my thinking, I began to dream. If I knew I could not fail in this business that was germinating in my mind, what would my ultimate goal be?

Most businesses, my research told me, were ripe for sale in seven years. And since Mrs. Smith's was the pie industry leader, my ultimate goal was easy to see: I would sell this pie business to Mrs. Smith's Bakeries in seven years. All I had to do was develop a product they were missing — which later emerged as the thaw-and-sell apple pie — in order to help them further dominate their marketplace. And that is exactly why they bought my business, six years and ten months later.

Although many people have pie-in-the-sky dreams — and *having* those big dreams is the crucial first step to making them a reality — you must move forward from there with concrete planning. What that meant for me was creating a series of goals that led up to my biggest objective — selling the company to Mrs. Smith's. To illustrate this process, I'll relate it to an event that has touched nearly everyone at some time in their life: planning a wedding.

I choose this analogy because my wife, Cindy, and I had been through that experience several years earlier, and the process fascinated me. I now see that it was my training ground for planning the success of my pie business. The first step in planning a wedding is to set a date for the event — the moment when all your planning comes together. Then you just work backward from that moment to create a series of goals, with a timeline for each goal, building to the ultimate event. Next, you create action steps that lead to each smaller goal, and from those you construct daily and weekly to-do lists.

As you work backward through this process to arrive back at your starting point (there's that circle again), you have your marching orders, broken into a long, well-thought-out series of "to-dos" that, once completed, will lead to your big goal. With this simple, but thorough, planning in place, you can easily see how many and what kind of people you will need, what skill sets will make each goal happen on time, and how much money you will need to accomplish each step. As you achieve each goal, your momentum builds, and you move farther and farther down the big timeline to that ultimate moment — the realization of your dream.

# Be Childlike When Defining Your Dream

Another necessary component of Infinite Persistence is to remember to have fun. With every part of even the toughest climb, the longest hours, the most grueling schedule, make sure that you always find a way to make it enjoyable.

From the moment you begin planning your journey, employ the childlike part of you that still loves to have fun. What was it that captivated you as a child? What did you enjoy doing more than anything? What did you tell everyone you wanted to be when you grew up? These questions, allowed free romp in your imagination, will help you define your dream. Allow yourself to believe that it's all possible — regardless of your age, what you are doing now, or where you live. Imagine that you can achieve whatever you dream. Create a new mindset that if you focus on your strengths and infinitely persist, whatever you dream of will be yours.

Our potential is as individual as the fingerprints we were born with, something we can draw upon throughout our lives to meet the challenges that move us toward our dreams. Sometimes we lose sight of the uniqueness of our own potential as we grow into adulthood. Think about the children in your life, and how their imaginations have no limitations. They *know* they can do or be or achieve anything they truly want, if only they want it badly enough. As we get older, through life's unexpected trials, we often begin to see only the obstacles, which we regard as limitations, that keep us from the success we dream of.

Eventually, as adults, we start to believe that our very potential has limits, so we begin to lose hope — and our innate awareness of what we can do if we persist as if those external limitations are not there. By integrating the concept of Infinite Persistence into our lives, we can rediscover the potential within us.

Have you ever noticed the uniqueness of a child's enthusiasm? Children have a lot to teach us about living with unbridled enthusiasm and excitement from moment to moment. Sure, there are disappointments, but for a child, the buoyancy of enthusiasm and energy quickly balances out even the most disappointing of events. In most cases, all it takes for children to shake off negative feelings is a simple explanation or just a little extra kindness from those around them. Living with childlike enthusiasm is key to working and achieving beyond what your adult mind accepts as possible and exploring your own unique, infinite potential.

Building on the resilience of childlike enthusiasm and being childlike in your business and life pursuits also means embracing spontaneity. Children are ready for a new adventure at the drop of a hat. And, if plans change, they are still on board — even if it takes a minute for them to regroup. If, as adults, we have forgotten how to be spontaneous, we need to relearn that skill in order to begin reclaiming our innate, childlike sense of our own potential.

Another important lesson on the path to Infinite Persistence that we can learn from our children is awareness. Kids are so aware of their surroundings that they notice many of the things that pass adults by without the slightest recognition. To truly reach for our infinite potential, we must remember how to really notice all that is happening around us. If we create the habit of noticing these details — of the events, and the people we come into contact with — we'll be better prepared to make the decisions that could dramatically affect our outcomes. Increasing our awareness is a tremendous help in dealing with the human element in ways that are necessary, productive, and significant to our success.

Approaching your life and your work with a childlike sense of adventure — reclaiming your earliest imagination, enthusiasm, and awareness — can be learned, whether you are 6 or 60. It's just a matter of knowing that it is possible — and pursuing it with Infinite Persistence.

The result? You will find yourself in places and with people your adult mind would never have thought possible. You will experience one-of-a-kind events that will drive you crazy with excitement, crazy with sheer challenge, and crazy with fun. And there may be moments when you will think that you are just plain crazy. But then you will realize how incredibly amazing your journey has been — and that it was your childlike approach that propelled you to a new threshold of infinite opportunity.

## The Teeter-Totter Effect — Creating the Balance for Success

Now, after you have given your childlike imagination space to play, it is equally important to create balance with some sound, adult thinking and planning when it comes to execution. The first part of this is discipline. As children, discipline is not something that we consider any fun. But as adults, we know that without discipline we cannot ever reach our potential.

Many of us mistakenly equate discipline with "punishment." The way out of this worn-out thinking is to find new ways to discipline ourselves that will put our exciting plans into place and help us follow them to meet our goals and realize our dreams. It can be as simple as making a list of things that we know we can finish by the end of each day. Just taking that first step of building discipline into your dreams and plans will launch your journey to a new reality.

## Make Friends With Time

To achieve infinite performance, you will need to learn how to invest and balance your time. This crucial step begins with the realization that time is your friend — not an enemy to be fought and conquered. If you can begin to view time as your friend and a playmate, you will unlock the door to infinite performance and be poised for success.

But once you decide to reframe time as your friend, what then? First you will need to establish a way to balance your time that works for you. Because we are all unique, this is something you will have to discover on your own, but like diets, exercise programs, and religion, just find something that works for you and stick to it. Whether it is making lists or delegating, fancy electronic gizmos or plain old pencil and paper, create your own system of efficiency — really just a balance of how you choose to spend your time — that will help you create your success.

## Get Off the Roller Coaster for Clearer Communication

Another important sense of balance you'll need to create in order to put a firm foundation underneath the castles you have allowed your childlike imagination to build is a solid ability to communicate effectively. To do this well you will need to learn to create balance in your emotions and your reactions. Whatever the situation, whatever may happen, whatever may come your way on any given day, be prepared to deal with it evenly — without the out-of-bound emotions of a disappointed child. This comes down to a simple matter of choice. You can do it; it just takes practice.

Think back to a situation in your life that upset you and caught you off guard — one in which you did not react with balance. Now consider how much better — and easier — the situation could have been resolved if you had reacted without the distraction of those strong emotions. What if you had taken a few minutes to step back and consider the best course of action rather than blowing up or allowing yourself to be overwhelmed with feelings of fear and failure? Each time you go through these scenarios, even in your mind, you are building new thought patterns and processes — dress rehearsals for the next time the real thing jumps up and challenges you. As with any new skill, the more you practice developing this new sense of balance, the stronger it will get.

Be deliberate in how you handle — and allow yourself to be affected by — the highs and lows of your journey. That doesn't mean you can't enjoy the excitement when things are going well — or feel the disappointment when things don't go as you wish — but shake these peaks and valleys off as quickly as you can. It is far better for your ultimate outcome if you can keep your emotions balanced, rather than allowing them to toss you about on their high or low tides. Your behaviors, reactions, and decisions will always be constructive if you train yourself to remember this key strategy of balance.

After you have achieved good habits of internal balance in dealing with time, focus, and emotions, it is time to consider the other skill sets you will need in order to propel your dream into reality. After a thorough and honest assessment of your own strengths and weaknesses, you will then be ready to pull together the people you will need to create a balance of skills that will enable you to accomplish each goal on your path to success — on time, on budget, and with a playful ease you never before dreamed possible.

## If You Build It, They Will Come — Creating a Team That Groks Your Dream

Once you have established the goals and recreated them in your mind as reality, it's time to share your dream with others. In 1961 a great new word was introduced to the world by author Robert Heinlein in the book *A Stranger in a Strange Land.* The word, "grok," according to *The American Heritage Dictionary,* means "to understand profoundly through intuition or empathy." Or in layman's terms, to really, really get it. If you recognize and recruit people who grok your dream, the combined intuitive understanding of a group will create an energy that cannot be ignored.

Have you ever been part of a team? If you have, you already know how the collective talents, abilities, and creativity of each person affect the entire outcome of a project. Every person brings something different to the table that benefits the whole. Align yourself with like-minded people who understand the power of *"never giving up, no matter what"* AND who possess the skill sets that you need to move your business forward along your timeline. Then, as I found out — and it took me several painful lessons to learn this, but I'll give it to you here, pain-free — it is crucial that you stay focused on *your* areas of strength while allowing others to support your dream with *their* strengths.

Meeting the right people at the right time can change your life, and, with Infinite Persistence, you'll be amazed at the synchronicity of these connections along the way. This is a very strong point to remember. When your intent is clear and strong, and the timing is right, the right people will show up. Believe it, know it, and expect them; they'll be there when you need them.

Creating a team of these key people can accomplish a dream that otherwise may not have been attainable. When you capture the imagination of others and they grok what you're trying to achieve, the combined belief, the strength of teamwork and collective Infinite Persistence will make the critical difference in meeting your ultimate goal.

## Replace Fear With Confidence

Fear is a tangible obstacle that creates resistance to the natural flow toward success. It can paralyze you, and your resulting indecision can rob you of your dreams. But when you replace fear with confidence, you will move ahead without resistance; the more confidence you gain, the more the positive momentum will build.

The question most likely on your mind now is "but how do I *do* that?" Some define fear as "false evidence appearing real." And at times, what you fear may appear more real than your dream, and dread can overshadow any progress you have made. Replacing fear with confidence requires effort on your part, but the rewards will be sweet. Meet each challenge head on, and keep repeating the Infinite Persistence mantra "*never give up, no matter what,*" regardless of how you feel. Stay focused on smaller goals that pave the way to your dream, and your confidence will increase exponentially. The accomplishment of each goal on the path to your dream will seal that feeling of confidence in your mind, and you will be able to draw upon it as you pursue your next challenge.

**"Our deepest fear is not that we are inadequate, but that we are powerful beyond measure. There's nothing enlightening about shrinking so that other**

**people won't feel secure around you. As we let our own light shine, we unconsciously give others permission to do the same."**

*— Nelson Mandela*

And it's not really the overanalyzed, super-clichéd "fear of failure" we need to worry most about. What you need to be more on guard against is that creeping, insidious detriment to progress known as "fear of success." Often the more difficult fear to deal with than failure (with failure you just keep getting back up and trying again), fear of success presents a much bigger challenge. You have to change your thinking.

The power of our thoughts to change the structure of our reality is demonstrated in the work of Masaru Emoto, a Japanese scientist and researcher, who, in a series of well-documented and highly scrutinized experiments, showed how the power of people's thoughts could change the very structure of molecules of water. In samples of polluted water taken from a lake in Japan, groups of people gathered and sent the water messages of love and positive affirmation. Before and after photographs of these molecules show the water to be transformed from mottled and murky blobs to crystalline structures reminiscent of snowflakes. This raised a question for everyone the world over who has come into contact with Emoto's experiments: If the power of people's thoughts can change the very structure of water, and our bodies are made of 70 percent water, what can changing our thinking do for us — and for our world?

Changing your ideas of success from a faraway, pie-in-the-sky dream to a reality you can get your arms around requires a shift in perspective that takes disciplined thinking. The good news is that the more you practice actively replacing fearful thoughts of "what if" with the calm assurance of your Infinite Persistence mantra, "*I will never give up, no matter what*," success, like failure, just becomes part of the puzzle, a teacher that leads you to the next part of your journey toward the achievement of your dream.

# Remember Your Successes to Build Infinite Layers of Persistence

To live a life of Infinite Persistence, it's necessary to take a solid stance in your own strength and power. This plays right back into the concept of controlling the quality of your thinking. (See? The circles are everywhere!) To take this approach, remember all that you have done and can do, and project these skills and successes forward to your future ventures.

As you attain each of the goals that comprise a step of your journey, you'll probably find that many types and levels of persistence will be required to make it to the top. Some of these challenges may be physically exhausting, like extensive travel. (My time aboard the Piebus on the Pie à la Road Tour was physically grueling beyond anything I could have imagined — it eventually even resulted in my need for back surgery!) Sometimes the layer of Infinite Persistence you are in will be a mental or emotional — even spiritual — challenge.

You can experience these different kinds of challenges — and varying shades of intensity — all at once or in any combination with every step you take on your journey. To create an attitude of Infinite Persistence throughout the many layers of challenges, stand tall in the belief of your dream and keep moving forward.

# Make Your Journey Worth the Effort

Applying the philosophy of Infinite Persistence to the entrepreneurial process creates a model of success that is clear, thoughtful, powerful, and real. Your primary mission then, regardless of your business or where you are in it, is to keep persisting, to keep moving ahead — and *never give up, no matter what.*

I've been on the rim of the black hole of uncertainty and doubt in my business, reaching out to grab the edge. I've reached out to try new things and gotten knocked back, only to catch my breath and reach out again, never giving up. Infinite Persistence is all about facing those hard knocks, rejection after rejection, and still moving ahead at whatever speed is possible. One step at a time, one inch at a time — or some days — one minute at a time. Just keep your momentum moving forward, knowing in your core that it is all part of your grand journey to the achievement of dreams that most people dare not even imagine.

In this paradigm shift, you truly can do anything you choose to do — if you are willing to do the work it takes and persist until you get to the edge of that hole, then to the ground above it. With each small success, you celebrate for a moment, then step back out there again to begin the next part of your journey, moving on to the next challenge. Persist infinitely and you will tap into the power of the Universe and achieve a new reality for your business.

# Infinite Persistence Is All About:

- believing in yourself and your dream

- making the choice to *never give up, no matter what*

- accomplishing whatever you choose to focus your time and attention on

- seeing the positive always and learning from your mistakes

- knowing that the challenges will lead you to a level of success that will exceed your expectations

- learning how to balance your life, while still pursuing your goals

- creating a level of awareness and a state of mind that motivates and allows you, the dreamer, to accomplish goals from a solid foundation

- accepting change as a partner to success

- reaching out until you can grab the prize — and then keep on moving

- designing your own journey to success

- making applesauce out of bruised apples and lemonade out of lemons

Believe in your dreams, infinitely persist, trust your instincts and *jump for that ring*. With Infinite Persistence, you can make it yours. Infinite Persistence is about seeing the sun when the clouds are out. It's about being unrelenting and about going just one more step. No matter what the obstacles, no matter what anyone says, with Infinite Persistence you can kick your way out of the box created by your own limitations and move forward to success. Infinite Persistence is about moving forward step by step, minute by minute to discover infinite possibilities.

**"Cherish your vision and your dreams as they are the children of your soul; the blueprints of your ultimate achievements."**

*— Napoleon Hill*

# CHAPTER 5

# My Own Story of Pi(e)

Let me start by telling my story. I've always believed that apple pie is the Great American Dessert. My great-grandma's secret recipe for apple pie was something very special, but also very simple, teaching me first how something could be so special and so simple at the same time. As a kid, I remember looking forward to one of Great-Grandma's apple pies with great anticipation. Apple pie always meant that the family was all together. It didn't have to be a holiday for us to get an apple pie, but it sure made the day feel like one. Eating a piece of her pie was like having Thanksgiving or Christmas dinner more than once a year. It was this feeling that created my desire to pursue a dream of having my own pie company. If she were still with us, I think she would use her favorite expression and say, "The apple doesn't fall very far from the tree!" I stopped counting the times she said that!

Every August, towns all over New Hampshire organize an event called "Old Home Day." In Londonderry, it's a giant town fair that starts off with a five-mile run at dawn, followed by a rousing parade filled with decorated floats, people, and bands. Next, the entire town turns out for a fair on the town common, complete with a band shell, where all day long local organizations from the Cub Scouts to the fire department make presentations to a grand audience. It is a quintessential American experience that everyone should have at least once in their lives.

In 1991, I won a blue ribbon in a pie-baking contest at the town fair in Londonderry, using my great-grandma's secret recipe for apple pie. This came as quite a shock to the other entrants, because here I was, a 6-foot, 9-inch, 27-year-old guy. On a dare from my friends and family, I entered again in 1992 to defend my title, and I won again! I still have both of those blue ribbons. This was the beginning of my journey to the achievement of a dream I hadn't even thought of yet.

*Slice of the Pi(e): Continue to build on your dream as you surpass each new challenge. As you honor each triumph, keep building more platforms for future success. Celebrate with amazement as you watch your dream grow.*

With this second victory, I figured the pie gods (and Great-Grandma) were smiling down at me and telling me it was time for apple pie to reclaim its title as the Great American Dessert. So, following my gut instincts and my heart, I defined my goals. In 1994, I decided to take the biggest risk of my life and start a company. I named — and branded — my company Gordon's Pies. My mom helped me with this — her maiden name was "Gordon." It was great that it was my name, too.

*Seed of Success: Invest the time in yourself and your dream. Take the time to define the goals and the steps necessary to get there. Then trust your instincts; they will lead you in the right direction. Consider that research and data are important, but allow your instincts to be your guide. Not everyone will agree or understand, but following your internal guidance system will keep your actions aligned with your conscience.*

To move my new company from dreams to reality, I first figured out what excites me and what I love to do. Then I shared my dream with my family and friends, and I had their support and encouragement from the very beginning.

The idea of starting my own business wasn't foreign to me or even that difficult to consider. Growing up, like most other kids, I had a passion, but it wasn't for baseball, stamp collecting, or the usual hobbies kids generally pursue. My passion was for business. I was always the kid in the neighborhood with the lemonade stand; I had a bicycle repair shop in my garage. Later on in college, I had my own window-washing business. I liked the feeling of meeting a challenge head on, and figuring out how to get from point A to point Z in the most direct way. I liked making money and the feeling of accomplishment that it brought. I also realized very early on in my business ventures that I had a great capacity to promote whatever I chose to do or chose to sell.

***Slice of the Pi(e):*** *Commit to living a life of passion, with enthusiasm in your heart. This will give you the mindset and energy to keep persisting and pursuing your goals. Feel it, breathe it, live it. Know that your dream is what you truly want; it's your passion in life.*

As a kid, I set up my lemonade stand in a handcrafted fire truck that my dad had built. And I used my unusual height to promote my window-washing business. Who wouldn't want a tall guy to wash their windows? It was all part of the package. I always looked for ways to get the attention of people and potential customers. I am a born marketer and public relations expert. Getting people's attention was both good business and big fun for me. I realized that if I was having fun, my dream and the money were always just right around the corner.

***Seed of Success:*** *Market creatively. Find a way to portray you and your product or service in a way that captures attention. Be "loud," literally and figuratively. Be magical! Shine your light! And have fun along the way, because fun always equals eventual success. People love to have fun. It's one of the most important components of a successful endeavor. Through your marketing and creative efforts, find a way to make it fun for you, for the people in your life, and for the people who will become your customers.*

Looking back, I realize that capitalizing on my natural strengths allowed me to pursue and achieve my dream.

But first I had to really analyze what my strengths were and what part they could play in meeting the goals I had set for myself. Keeping the focus on my strengths, I found the ride could be much smoother — and much more fun. I rediscovered this truth again and again as my path to success unfolded before me.

My parents were always my biggest supporters, my mentors, and my positive role models. My dad was a pediatrician. My mom, an educator, became the preeminent consultant on mentoring in the country. As I grew up, my folks always encouraged me to follow my dreams, and they told me that I could do anything and be anything I wanted to be. There were no limits or boundaries on what they believed I could do. The confidence I gained from my parents' belief in me cannot be underestimated. I drew on that early learning experience throughout the pursuit of my dream and believed in it. I have since passed that belief on to my own kids, Emily, Jack, and Sam, every day. My hope is that as adults they will be able to say that my belief in them helped enrich their lives and enable them see their own infinite potential and achieve their biggest dreams.

Think about the person or people who have believed in you, encouraged you, and told you that you can do anything you choose to do. You have to believe that there is nothing you cannot be, nothing you cannot do, and nothing you cannot have if you work hard enough and persist without fear. Our capacity for Infinite Persistence grows from our beliefs in our own infinite potential.

But that doesn't mean it is going to be easy. Even with my folks telling me that I could do anything and be anything I wanted to be, I struggled. In grade school, I was tracked as one of the kids who would never excel. Thankfully, my parents refused to believe that. They found a tutor, Dr. Degnan, who helped me learn the art of organizing my thoughts and work habits. I have used those tools I learned in the sixth grade throughout my entire life. These work habits changed my life and have been a significant factor of my success. In fact, the skills I learned from Dr. Degnan enabled me to define my dream and to learn how to pursue it — and eventually to make it reality.

*Seed of Success: Allowing others to per-form tasks that relate to their skills is important, but focusing on your own strengths will further your success. First, determine what comes naturally to you, your talents, skills, and abilities — what flows through you without a struggle, what you are truly good at. Use those abilities to work toward your dream.*

## Lean on Your Strengths and Shore up Your Weaknesses

For my pie company, I decided that I wanted to create and develop a brand that customers could identify with, like Ben & Jerry's ice cream, Samuel Adams beer or Cape Cod Potato Chips. I was especially impressed with an entrepreneur named Frank Purdue after learning how much time he spent in butcher shops, and later in grocery stores, shaking hands and promoting his Purdue brand of chicken long before there was such a thing as branded chicken. Frank Purdue was not only personable, but he also had a talent for getting people's attention. By taking the time to meet people and get their attention, Frank Purdue was able to build enthusiasm for his brand and achieve customer loyalty.

I studied the loyalty-building strategies of Frank Purdue and countless others, and I learned these lessons well. In business and in life, loyalty is vital. Without it, I could not have made steady progress, achieved commitment, or moved past the hurdles. Enthusiasm builds loyalty that can't be shaken, even when the wind blows the tree so hard that you think the last apple will fall from its branch.

***Seed of Success:*** *Build loyalty with customers, vendors, and employees through your actions. Show them that you are who you say you are by doing what you say you will do. Loyalty also creates priceless word-of-mouth publicity that will sell your dream much more effectively and much less expensively than advertising. Advertising and marketing are important, but so is how your* *product is perceived by the people who pay for it or work to help create it.*

My dream was to brand my great-grandma's apple pie recipe, but at that time, I was still working at a Boston-based public relations firm earning a good salary. On March 29, 1994, I came home from work and asked my wife, Cindy, whom I always refer to as my pie angel in honor of her unwavering support, if she would support my decision to take this risk to go for my dream. I wanted to leave my job and start the Top of the Tree Baking Company, Inc. to begin making Gordon's Pies. Cindy, who was an occupational therapist, agreed to take on the challenge and, for the next three years, she totally supported our family financially and emotionally. She became my first key team member who went the distance and adopted my dream as her own.

Success really is all about belief in a dream, not just by the dreamer, but also by the people most directly affected by the work that goes into pursuing the dream. Without my sense of belief — and the support of my family and my friends — when my company began, I would have had nothing to build upon. Building my company on this collective belief was the foundation for realizing my dream.

## Define Your Dream, and Then Create the Steps to Achieve It

William James, the father of American psychology, wrote that there are three rules to follow if you want to change your life: start immediately, do it flamboyantly, and remember that there are no exceptions. These three rules create a sense of urgency, an air of drama, and a level of commitment that will propel you to grow and change and reach your goals. I decided to take his advice.

For the next nine months of 1994, I talked to everyone I could about starting a food business. I called and spoke with people from Mrs. Smith's Bakeries, Sara Lee, Table Talk and Comstock Pie Fillings. Every day, I spoke with grocery store managers, bakery managers and entrepreneurs all over the United

States. I've often been asked why these people took the time to talk with me. It's really simple. I picked up the phone and asked them questions. Like they say, "Ask and you shall receive!"

Some of the best advice I ever received was from Steve Bernard, founder of Cape Cod Potato Chips. He told me that despite what anyone's expertise claimed, ultimately, "You need to put your own sweat into it; no one will do that for you." I found out very soon how prophetic his words were.

*Slice of the Pi(e)*: *Define your dreams with straightforward, simply stated goals and believe in them without fear, no matter what. Know that you accomplish what you believe you can, and you become who you believe you can be.*

# Market Research: Find the Problem, and You've Found Your Opportunity

Every problem is an opportunity for a creative solution that will propel you up the ladder of success. As I did my research to help me identify the need in my market, I found out (by reading everything I could get my hands on about the local market and calling all the leaders in the grocery store industry) that the labor force in grocery stores was getting tighter and scarcer all the time. This limited labor force was dramatically reducing the amount of products that could be baked in the grocery stores. This especially included pies. My thaw-and-sell pie was a huge time-saving product and provided a very creative solution to this problem. Fully baked at factory level, instantly frozen, and then shipped to the grocery store, my pies only had to thaw for a few hours before in-store bakery personnel could simply put them on their shelves for sale to their customers.

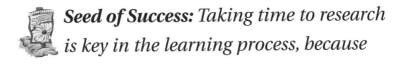 ***Seed of Success:*** *Taking time to research is key in the learning process, because*

*information discovered enhances the end result. Know your market. Research your competitors, gather information, and go to the source. Talk to people and ask for their advice. You'll be surprised at what they'll tell you. Some-times, all you have to do is ask. To gather information about your market and your competitors, go to the source. You'll probably be surprised how many people will answer your questions — all you have to do is ask. This is how you can really know your market. With this approach to market research, your decisions will be based on the answers you get to the questions you have — and what your instincts tell you about those answers.*

## Build Loyalty to Create Your Brand

As I continued to research the pie business, I was baking all the Gordon's Pies, first in my kitchen and then at a local bakery. Cindy and I would package the pies with a little brochure describing my story, and I would deliver the pies three times a week out of the back of my car to a local apple orchard in Londonderry called Mack's Apples. I also sold and delivered pies to small grocery stores throughout New Hampshire and Massachusetts. At the same time, I was also promoting my business like crazy, giving away my three-pound apple pies and Gordon's EAT MO' PIE!® T-shirts all over New Hampshire and Massachusetts. It really left an impression on everyone. These early promotions also reinforced the concept I had about building my personality-based brand. My strengths — my skills in marketing and public relations — played an important part. Reaching out to people in this way built enthusiasm with customers who would come back again and again. I found out firsthand that who you are and how you present yourself affects customers' perceptions of your product or service. Your brand is built on your customers' perceptions of who you are and reinforced by the quality of your product or service. It's another circle that builds on itself, creating power and momentum as your customer base grows, both in numbers and in loyalty.

***Seed of Success:*** *Brand yourself — and your dream. This means, put simply, that you work to not only market your product, but also to create an exciting presence that will continue to pull people toward you and your dream, independent of the product you sell. To do this, use your skills and talents and be willing to take your creativity as far as you can — and then further. Find a way to be different. Think about what captures your interest and apply it to your product or service. Promote quality in all you do — and not just product quality, although a quality product is crucial to success and longevity in any market. Continue to enhance the quality of your ideas, your concepts, your strategies, and your goals — as well as the systems you have created for reaching them.*

## Create Boundless Enthusiasm

To create boundless enthusiasm for your dream, you first have to find a way to say, "Here I am!" Use your marketing strategies to bring attention to your product or service, whether that is through the Internet, advertising, word of mouth, or publicity stunts. It's all about uniqueness. Be outrageous!

# Make Dollar Profits in a Penny Business

The food business is not an easy one and I had no experience, so what an education I got! I came to find out that it's what is called a "penny business," meaning there is not much profit for grocery store operators in food, even though the typical grocery store carries more than 30,000 products. This is the part of the story where I had to rely on the strength of my convictions.

All I really knew for sure was that I had a winner recipe for apple pie that would succeed. The naysayers said, "Customers won't like your product; there is no room on the shelf for your brand; the big companies will squeeze you out if you have any success." I heard all those things they had to say and it all amounted to a resounding, "Don't do it!" But I knew I had the solution grocers were looking for. They just didn't know it yet.

On March 29, 1994, the day I decided to start my company, I promised myself that no matter what happened, I would not give up. I said it out loud. "I will not give up." I said it several times, over and over. I wrote it down. I said it again. "I will not give up." That promise to myself has gotten me through the most trying of times on so many different occasions. But even more, that simple vow began germinating within me the key to my — and your — success. It was the beginning of my awareness of the power of Infinite Persistence. **The most important ingredient of Infinite Persistence is:** *never give up, no matter what!*

*Slice of the Pi(e): Keep it simple. Keep a clear picture in your mind of what you want to accomplish. It's right there in your imagination. Find it, refine it, and revisit it often. Write it down. Say it out loud.*

*"Your vision is your passion, and your passion creates your vision."* — *D. Ford*

# Be Insightful in Your Marketing

Another thing that became clear early in my research was that I needed to market my apple pie differently. Until my creation of Gordon's Pies, the only place you could buy a branded pie was the frozen food section of the grocery store. That's where Mrs. Smith's pies are sold.

The only other place to market my product, as far as I could tell, was the in-store bakery. That's where you can buy freshly baked bread, cookies, and éclairs, and even have your mom's birthday cake decorated. Pies are also sold in the in-store bakery, but I quickly realized that nothing was branded, except with the name of the grocery store. My marketing insight was that I knew the in-story bakery was the place for my pies. I just had to figure out how to market that insight to my prospective customers.

For the most part, unlike your mom, supermarkets do not make anything completely from scratch. Instead, other companies make and supply products for the supermarkets. These products are often shipped frozen, thawed out, and then placed on the supermarket's shelves. This concept of manufacturing for supermarkets is called co-packing. I might have been new to the food business, but I wasn't entirely naïve. I could plainly see that if the ultimate customer did not know they were biting into a Gordon's Apple Pie, how could I build a brand and, more important, what prevented the supermarket from discontinuing my pie when some other company offered them a better deal?

Although I was a financial novice, my marketing savvy kicked in, and I knew I could not market an unbranded commodity product. Because there were no other branded products in the in-store bakery, I saw a huge opportunity to get my pies in front of the customer in an untapped section of the supermarket. I believed I could make my branded pie an impulse item in the in-store bakery.

With this idea firmly in place, next I searched for open spaces for this new concept in the pie market to find the grocery store buyers who would relate to my dream. As I looked at each prospective store, I asked myself, "How would my product fit there? How could I break through to my chosen area in a better or different way? Where is *my* piece of the pie?"

*Seed of Success: Keep researching. Be aware of how your product or service is perceived by your customers. Be aware of the new possibilities or trends in the marketplace. Look at what is out there, and then engage your talents and the talents of your team to take advantage of this information to keep your thinking out front and ahead of your competition.*

# All About Branding

Although I had no formal marketing training after majoring in sociology at Bowdoin College in Brunswick, Maine, I had always known that I wanted to someday brand a product. The technical definition of branding is the establishment and nurturing of an enduring, distinct, or, best of all, unique impression in the minds of customers. Building a brand means carving a niche in the marketplace through price, quality, service, or some combination of the three.

The way I figured it, if customers liked my brand, I would sell more pie and, in turn, build customer loyalty that would strengthen my brand. Developing this kind of brand loyalty meant that customers would come along with me as trends changed and as I developed new products. In addition, I learned that the more customers appreciated the uniqueness of my brand — and the quality it promised — the more they were willing to pay for my brand's products. Cases I studied to research this process were Ben & Jerry's ice cream, Samuel Adams beer and Purdue chicken. Each of these brands commanded a premium price in the marketplace because they constantly delivered on their promise to provide a high-quality product — and because they were in some way recognized by their consumers as unique.

Ultimately, a brand is a relationship, and customer experiences shape that brand. I learned that customers are smart and savvy, and they can always tell the difference between a true identity and marketing fluff. I knew the key to ringing true with my customers was to always exceed their expectations. Although my marketing approach is somewhat unconventional, I have always made sure it reflects my company's core values: quality, integrity, respect, honesty, and trust. And since the beginning of Gordon's Pies, my pie-loving customers have recognized these values and have rewarded me with their loyalty to the brand I created.

Although I didn't know all of the jargon when I decided to start my company, I knew I was extremely loyal to particular products and companies, and I wanted to create the same feelings with folks who swapped their hard-earned dollars for a Gordon's Pie. Letter after letter and phone call after phone call have proven that the Gordon's brand has indeed created and fostered this kind of customer enthusiasm, and enthusiasm is what nurtures branding success.

***Seed of Success:*** *Practice "in your face" marketing. Infinite performance requires capturing the fortress and winning the battle by getting in the eye-view or face of your audience. Show people you are who you say you are. Show the people you work with and the people you sell to — whether it be a service or a product — that you will stand behind what you say, and communicate this through all of your marketing and presentation efforts.*

# Finding the Right Location

My original dream was to brand Gordon's Pies and to build a Willy Wonka-style factory right in my hometown of Londonderry. Cindy and I had moved to Londonderry from Boston after I graduated from Bowdoin College and after she had graduated from Boston University. Like most young couples, we couldn't afford to live in Boston proper, so we moved the hour north into New Hampshire.

Today, Londonderry is a beautiful little town of 22,000 residents. In 1994, the town had half that population. The schools were great, there was no crime to speak of, and, best of all, there were five apple orchards to make my main ingredient. With an ample supply of juicy apples readily available, it was the perfect place to begin an apple pie business.

Having done public relations in Boston right out of college, I recognized the gold mine of an opportunity that went along with my idea for the factory. I could buy my apples from the local orchards, buy my flour from a local miller, employ local folks in my factory, and even invite kids to tour the factory. The Town of Londonderry and the New Hampshire Department of Agriculture were wonderfully supportive of my new venture. These folks loved the fact that I was promoting Londonderry and its apple industry. For them, it would mean more jobs, commerce, and recognition. For me, it meant moving my dream forward with invaluable local support.

## Finding Funding

While excitement on its own can get a project off the ground, it will not pay for the equipment and the facility necessary to open and run a factory. By my calculations, I needed an additional $75,000 after my $50,000 Small Business Administration loan and the $100,000 line of credit from my local banker at the Bank of New Hampshire. I began looking for investors in the form of friends and family members. I soon found out that one of the hardest things to do in business is to ask for money. I ended up with eleven friends and family members who, in 1994, invested a total of $75,000 in me and my dream. Yes,

I had a company and would soon have a factory and many Pieteam members, but ultimately, these folks invested in me and the belief I had in my dream. I took that responsibility very seriously. The agreement with my initial investors was that they were entitled to double their money in six years.

***Seed of Success:*** *Solicit investors who are enthusiastic about your dream. Market your idea in a way that will entice them and seize their attention in such a way that they will not be able to say no. With a great product or service and an eye-catching plan for promoting it, you will gain the enthusiasm for investors to believe in your dream.*

I used the bank and the investment dollars to build my factory. Not surprisingly (in retrospect, anyway) and due entirely to my own financial inexperience, the money ran out in less than one year. So I had started using my personal credit cards to make payroll and amassed around $30,000 in credit card debt. While it was a risk to use my own credit cards, my staff was incredibly loyal to me. It was critical for me to recognize their loyalty with my own.

***Seed of Success:*** *Loyalty to the people who help build your dream is an important thing to remember. Without your "dream team," you may not reach the peak. Having members with different talents and abilities will only add to your success.*

## Let the Media Carry Your Message

Despite my lack of financial experience, I was right about one thing. With my P.T. Barnum-type promotional efforts going full-steam, my Londonderry factory was a public relations gold mine. In fact, presidential candidates stopped there during their 1994 campaigns in our first-in-the-nation primary state. I was featured on the covers of *Fortune Small*

*Business, Entrepreneur, The Boston Globe Magazine,* and dozens of national publications and television shows. Public relations was my saving grace. Since I had no money for advertising, I needed a way to speak directly with customers, and this was my opportunity. My pie and T-shirt giveaways accomplished this agenda on a limited scale, and articles written by credible publications gave my story a wider distribution.

The magazine and newspaper stories also added fuel to my decision to develop and build a personality-based brand. I "put myself out there" in every interview. I decided that if I remained open and honest with the media, customers would respond in a supportive fashion. I was right. People responded in amazing ways to my forthright approach. I could see how much they appreciated dealing with someone who had integrity — someone who would tell them the truth. People want to know you're the real deal.

*Core Value: Be open and forthcoming; always be the first to initiate a call. Pursue your dream with integrity; be up front with everyone you deal with. Be real and always tell the truth, and people will believe you.*

## Live up to Your Buzz

While I was getting more than my fair share of media exposure in the New England market, I wasn't yet selling millions of pies. In fact, my marketing strategies had far outpaced my manufacturing and production capabilities. But by 1996, sales of Gordon's Pies totaled $400,000. I was pretty proud of this number, since I was spending virtually all my time supervising my manufacturing operations instead of focusing on my marketing and public relations abilities.

Despite all the positive publicity I was generating and moral support I was receiving, what I hadn't bargained for was that my quaint factory was turning out to be a money-burning, logistical nightmare. Costs far exceeded the income being produced by sales.

Manufacturing, even when done right, is a grueling business, and to compound this, we were operating with limited experience and an even more limited cash flow — not to mention that we were essentially a start-up business, which further complicated matters. I worked day and night and even slept on a couch in my office at the factory virtually every night, as did most of my senior staff members. I hated being away from my family, but this out-of-control thing that the pie factory had become required my constant and undivided attention.

Our operation was completely manual — not one part of our process was automated, right down to the apple-peeling machine, appropriately named Dudley. I was using ovens like you would find in your local pizzeria to bake my pies. And it was an extremely amateur operation. Dedicated, yes, but extremely amateur.

Despite the hardships of employing inexperienced temporary labor, which compounded my own incompetence, my experiences in running the factory eventually proved to be invaluable. Knowing how something should *not* be done can provide extraordinary insight — it's all a matter of perspective. A positive perspective and the ability to see where a process or concept needed to be changed saved my dream from crashing. The experience I gained allowed me to move past the challenge and reach even higher.

*Core Value: Meet each challenge head on; face squarely the hurdles you encounter. They are essential elements on your road to achievement. Celebrate challenges, because without them, there would be nothing to learn from and no turning points. It is the turning points that bring you success.*

## Packaging Perception

While running the factory was difficult, Gordon's Pies was continuing to develop quite a strong customer following, based in some part on my great-grandma's pie recipe, in some part on my marketing and public relations skills, and in other parts on my packaging. And to pull all this together I called upon my natural abilities as a storyteller.

Without any advertising budget whatsoever, I had to find ways to reach my customers as well as my potential customers without spending much money. That's what drove my determination to get publicity in any way possible. I realized early on the power of the written word, and that a news story told by a journalist was perceived as extremely credible by t he publication's readers and was the best advertising — and endorsement — I could possibly get. I knew I couldn't get into the newspaper or on a television program every single day, but that fact did not create any lack of trying on my part. That's where my brown pie box entered the picture; it became my signature packaging.

# Creating the Perfect Package

When I started my company, the pies in the in-store bakeries were sold in either clear plastic packaging or in thin, white bakery boxes. At most, there was a sticker applied at the store that gave pricing, nutritional details, and expiration information, but that's it. To me, the packaging offered a free billboard, an opportunity to tell my story to anyone who even *saw* my pies. From the advertising world I knew the value of imprinting your message on someone's brain, whether they buy your product or not. Even fleeting exposure plants a seed of recognition.

Also, I wanted the customer to buy my pie with their eyes. To accomplish this, I had a little strategy that worked extremely well. I chose a brown box with a see-through apple hole because it was the least expensive format available. And with the difference in size and color, and my message printed all over it, my pie boxes really stood out from their competition. It also became instantly clear to me, however, that customers identified my brown box as "more homey and earthy" than those of my competitors.

Plus, Gordon's Pies were more expensive, which most often resulted in a more homemade presentation on the grocer's shelves. Before I knew it, Gordon's Pies became known as the "pie in the big brown box."

Homing back in on the realization that manufacturing was not my forte, but that marketing and public relations were my true strengths, I began to fully grasp the power of communicating with customers through the packaging of my product — and my brand would be the key to my success. This realization helped me fully understand how important packaging is to your ultimate success. And, when you can establish this connection with your customers, they will speak of you favorably and speak of you often to their friends, families, and neighbors. Word of mouth can build just as strong a brand, if not stronger, than any form of traditional advertising.

***Seed of Success:*** *"Package" your dream in a unique, eye-catching way. It's all about presentation and perception. Do something different. In order to be recognized, your* *ideas or product will have to stand out from the crowd. Find a way to communicate how your product or service is unlike anything else out there.*

## The Thrills and Chills of Escalating Volumes

When it came to word of mouth, my appearances on QVC, the home shopping channel, were incredible for our sales. People still remember that I was on QVC three times, and that was seven years ago! The first time I was on QVC, we sold 3,000 pies in two minutes. We shipped the pies from the factory with the help of our good friends at UPS. Friends, neighbors, UPS executives, anyone we could ask, helped package and send the pies out all over the country. I learned the following lesson rather quickly: Don't ship out frozen high-dome pies if you don't know what you're doing!

This experience showed me how important it was to research everything to do with my product — even shipping. Shipping was one of the key factors of selling through QVC. I learned that I needed to focus on all aspects of a new, unfamiliar method of selling. It wasn't always necessary to learn the hard way.

## Analyzing Your Costs

In January 1997, time was running out on Gordon's Pies. My food technologist had informed me that not only were we not making money on each and every pie we were producing, we were, in fact, *losing* money. The most important part of any business is identifying costs. This exercise allows you to know how far away you are from turning a profit. I was horrible at that part of the financial equation. The fact that I was losing money was a rude awakening for me. I knew I wasn't getting rich on Gordon's Pies. In fact, I still had not taken a salary after being in business for more than two years. But losing money? Wow! At first, this development set me back emotionally. I didn't know what to think. How could I work so hard, spend all my waking and sleeping moments at the factory, and still be losing money? I was disheartened. I felt very let down by my financial advisors, and I was disappointed in myself. Plus, while I was spending all my time attempting to run the factory, my wife, Cindy, was working and running our household by herself. The sacrifices to my personal life were already starting to mount up, but it would take me a long time to recognize this. I realize now that this was the point in my story where balance, another aspect of the Infinite Persistence model, was beginning to reveal itself to me. But, again, it would take a long time for me to see it. I was too focused on producing and selling to pay attention to my personal life and what needed to be taken care of there. I didn't yet realize that it was all interconnected.

## Keep Your Focus Flexible

Despite my personal disappointment over not being able to run an efficient factory, I constantly reminded myself of the promise I made on Day One: I would not give up. I hadn't come this far and worked this hard to quit. Plus, I did not get into business to *survive*. My goal was to *thrive* in my marketplace. The only way I saw to remedy my financial predicament was to improve my pie-making abilities at the factory level and to buy freezer display units for installation in my supermarket customers' stores.

I was still intent on turning Gordon's Pies into an impulse item that people would buy on sight. Each of these freezer units would cost $500. I surmised that with increased efficiencies in production and display units at store level, I might actually start to make money with my brand. By my calculations, raising $1 million would mean that I could make my factory more "Willy Wonka" than Rube Goldberg (master of the exceedingly complex contraption). In retrospect, I now recognize this as the "throw-good-money-after-bad" strategy. I hadn't yet integrated the second tenet of Infinite Persistence: honest assessment. Without a brutally honest assessment of my financial condition, I was still operating with pie-in-the-sky expectations.

*Slice of the Pi(e): After each learning experience, assess yourself — your choices, your actions, your behavior, and your habits. This process will affect the direction of your dream, and often it will lead to important insights about where to focus your attention.*

At the time, though, I thought my expectations *were* reasonable. I didn't operate with a get-rich-quick mentality, and every decision I made was with the knowledge that I was responsible to my investors and to my bank. I was willing to work hard. I knew that the word entrepreneur wasn't necessarily a synonym for millionaire. The problem was that neither my advisors nor I had the experience to recognize when we were making mistakes. This was a critical area that needed to be tackled.

The big question at the time was "How can I raise $1 million?" Of course, where there's a will, there's a way. (I think this is a good place to say that, normally, I don't like to use clichés. I believe that many people hang on to clichés rather than adopting the behavior that forms the basis of the cliché.) My philosophy in business, however, supports the premise that if you truly believe in yourself — that is, if you are confident in your abilities to figure things out — you can find a creative solution to any problem. Raising $1 million was no different or more difficult than any of the other problems I had already faced and solved. To meet the $1 million challenge, I needed to create some positive exposure for my product and my brand that people would not forget.

## Hittin' the Pi(e) Trail

In the summer of 1995, I purchased a marketing tool for publicity and recognition — a 1983 International school bus — for $1,000. I painted it colorfully with my slogan, and christened it the "44-foot Piebus." I originally planned to use it for promotional events for Gordon's Pies, but it became a crucial part of my business recovery plan. The Piebus was nothing more than a school bus most kids still take today, except that it was louder, dirtier, and more uncomfortable to ride in.

The Piebus was very good at one thing, though. It was a magical-looking vehicle that provided an extremely colorful backdrop for getting people's attention, and it was unlike any vehicle anyone has ever seen. I removed all the interior seats and outfitted the inside with two desks, bunk beds, and a stand-up freezer, which first served as a cooler and then as a large file cabinet so we could work on the road. It was fun and, depending on your age, reminiscent of either Ken Kesey's Acid Kool-Aid Tour Bus or the Partridge Family bus.

No matter who climbed aboard the Piebus, from corporate CEO to six-year-old, it always evoked the same wide-eyed, incredulous reaction. The only music played on the Piebus was disco. It was amazing how it made everyone smile when they saw that crazy-looking, wildly painted Piebus blaring out its lively disco music! The Piebus lived up to and exceeded its charge to become our greatest marketing and public relations tool. It was my golden ticket to the Willy Wonka success I had first envisioned.

***Seed of Success:*** *Have fun along the way, because fun equals success. Create and build boundless enthusiasm for your dream and find a way to make it fun for you, the people in your life, and those who will become your customers. Find a way to say, "Here I am!" Use marketing to bring attention to your product or service via the Internet, advertising, word of mouth or publicity stunts. It's all about uniqueness. Be outrageous!*

# Raising a Million — Almost

In January 1997, together with three members of my Pieteam, I set out to raise $1 million from investors. In New Hampshire, you have to be certified by the State of New Hampshire to solicit investment, and you have to keep the prospectus documents with you as you travel around to raise money. I received my certification and set out on a cross-country trip toward my chosen destination — the First Annual Great American Pie Festival in Boulder, Colorado. Since I knew that Jim Koch had received national recognition in his launch of Samuel Adams beer by winning "Best Beer in America," I figured I could do the same thing at the American Pie Festival — plus, if I played my cards right, I could raise $1 million along the way. I was hoping to accomplish both of these lofty goals on my trip, so that when I returned home to Londonderry, not only would I have raised the money the company needed, but we also would have received important national recognition and even more publicity.

To pursue both of these goals, I had a long list of people I wanted to meet, and over the years I had developed a key theory to getting business done quickly: Go to the source if you want to get something done.

The aim of the American Pie Council (APC) is for pie-baking companies to come together and strategize ways to promote the pie business throughout the country. The APC is a trade organization run by two amazing people, Rich Hoskins and his wife, Linda. They also own Colborne Equipment

Company, which manufactures pie-baking equipment. Since I wanted to renovate and update my factory, and since the Hoskins sold equipment, they were definitely on my list of people to visit and get to know.

***Seed of Success:*** *Go to the source. At the most, it usually takes only two or three phone calls to find out who is in charge or who has the information you need. Test this theory. It can save you an incredible amount of time and frustration. I can't emphasize this enough. It works. It just works.*

When I left New Hampshire for Colorado in January of 1997, since my primary mission was to find investors, my Pieteam and I routed the Piebus through all the places where we thought rich people would meet and socialize. At our first stop, the Four Seasons Hotel in Boston, I valet-parked the Piebus and, with pies and T-shirts in hand, took over the cigar bar. There I met a high-ranking officer with Shearson Lehman American Express who loved my marketing ideas, and he pledged $300,000 on the spot. After just one day I had already raised $300,000! This put me on an incredible emotional high, but it was very early in the trip.

The trip to Colorado was fun, but grueling. By the time we arrived in Boulder, we were exhausted, and I had run up even more debt on my personal credit cards. And to add insult to that injury, Gordon's Pies didn't win any awards that year at the American Pie Festival. The pie business, I discovered, was as political as any other business. To make matters even worse, the Piebus broke down, both on the way to Colorado and on the way home. On the way home, we broke down in the little town of Pontiac, Illinois. The town took us under its wing and fed and entertained us until the Piebus was back in service. We still correspond with the people from Pontiac and will never forget their generosity. It's amazing how everyone you encounter becomes part of your journey toward a dream.

*Slice of the Pi(e): The power of the often inexplicable connection that exists between all people can be surprising, and it often shows up in the simplest of ways, such as the kindness of strangers toward the worn-out inhabitants of a broken-down Piebus.*

When we arrived back in New Hampshire, I was just $300,000 short of my $1 million goal. In order to protect investors, that license to raise money in the State of New Hampshire also requires that once an individual sets a target investment goal, he or she must raise at least that amount or give back all of the pledges.

So here I was, returning home, beat up and weary from a cross-country trek on a less-than-perfect Piebus. And I was still looking for that last $300,000. Employed in my pie factory were all sorts of characters, from local moms to ex-social workers. One factory worker we had grown very close to claimed that he had been left a small fortune when his parents died. He also was a member of the Pieteam that accompanied me on my trip to Colorado. Upon our return to New Hampshire, he told me that *he* would invest money from his inheritance to fund the remaining $300,000, which would allow me to reach my $1 million goal.

Needless to say, I was tremendously grateful for this generous gesture. With his investment, we would reach the $1 million goal, which would infuse badly needed cash into my ailing company. Without that money, I knew I would have to face options that I was not yet willing to consider.

Unfortunately, I was conned. There was no "fortune" to be had, and by making up this story — and the phony investment offer — this guy really had nothing to gain except my short-term appreciation. Upon investigation, Cindy and I discovered that nothing this guy had told us was true. We had taken this man not only into our home, but into our lives. The day I learned the truth, I went down to the factory and simply asked him to leave, immediately. I'll never forget that day. Appropriately, it was pouring rain; I remember the surreal moment as I looked out my second-story office window and watched him walk away in the downpour. I never saw or heard from him again. That experience took my innocence, plain and simple. But it created another turning point for me.

*Slice of the Pi(e): The world is made up of all kinds of people, and human nature is not always as straightforward as we would like for it to be. From this experience, I learned that people will do things that make no sense, for whatever reason, and we must not take these unexpected behaviors personally. Rather, know that experiencing the flip side of human nature always creates rich opportunities for unparalleled growth.*

But even worse than my personal disappointment, I was out of options for further pledges, so I had to give back all the money I had raised on the road trip to Colorado. I was devastated. Cindy and I took a drive with our kids up the Maine coast to figure out our options. We contemplated and discussed our future. Should we stick with the plan or should we take the huge con as a sign that it was time to leave the pie business and move on?

During this utterly dark time, the company had become a financial albatross around my neck. I had no money and had not manufactured or shipped a pie in almost four months. I was being counseled by my financial advisor and my lawyer to shut the doors and file for bankruptcy, both personally and for the business. After all, I was $800,000 in the hole on my balance sheet. At this time, I was still unsure what a balance sheet was, for that matter. I owed seventy-two local vendors about $400,000. I was three months behind on my payments to everyone, and the creditors and credit agencies were calling on a daily basis.

I was more depressed than I had ever been in my life. My dream of creating my fortune selling the Great American Dessert was in shambles. But bank-ruptcy was a devastating concept to me. While I knew, logically, that many companies and individuals filed for bankruptcy — and that there was no shame in it — my heart simply couldn't handle that scenario. Not only would my vendors probably not get anything close to what I owed them, but my investors would get nothing. For me, bankruptcy would have been giving up *and* failing to pay my investors. That idea made me sick to my stomach and wasn't an option in my mind. At the end of that weekend in Maine, I decided to delay the decision to file for bankruptcy.

*Core Value: If you find yourself experiencing too much emotional fluctuation — either a soaring high or a crashing low — it is a signal that you need to work on achieving emotional balance. As hard as it is, I now strive to discipline myself to stay on an even course emotionally. Living that way is much less exhausting and I am a much better thinker on every level.*

# When the Time Is Right, the Right People Appear

And as fate would have it, the pie gods were not ready to let my dream die. Every year, my parents hosted a family reunion week in Hilton Head, South Carolina, and one year, my sister's good friend, Pam, also came for a visit. Pam had been a bankruptcy lawyer in New York City before leaving four months earlier to coach college softball in Charleston, South Carolina. Pam and I started talking about the business and the state of my affairs. Her insights shed a new light on my predicament and gave me a new perspective. While I did owe a lot of money to a lot of people, in absolute terms, it really wasn't that much money. Pam gave me the confidence to remember that I had a truly great idea. She also reminded me that before they were my creditors, the folks I now owed money to were my vendors, and they had once believed in me and my dream. The critical challenge before me, then, was to remind my vendors of this fact. This was another instance where I had to meet a tough challenge head on and, again, *never give up, no matter what.*

Although the power of Infinite Persistence was still largely a mystery to me, I understood on a very deep level that I had to stay confident and persist at that time more than I ever had before.

***Slice of the Pi(e):*** *To wish for something is to be given the power to make it real. Desire is a way to persist with passion. Your heart and your soul will tell you what you desire, and from this, you will know the direction you are to take.*

Pam asked whether I had been in communication with my vendors or whether I was avoiding them. I assured her that I was not avoiding them. "Good," Pam replied, "because no matter how fast you try to run, your creditors can always run faster." On Pam's advice, I wrote a letter to all my creditors and explained where I was, financially. I told them right up front that I had been conned, but I was committed to paying them back the money I owed for the various goods and services they had provided, from apples to flour to cardboard. I asked each one of them for some time while I figured out my next move.

I am convinced that this up-front communication with my vendors saved Gordon's Pies. Basically, they had nothing to lose by giving me some time, because if I had to file for bankruptcy, they would have recovered nothing. In retrospect, this was a very prudent business decision for them. My commitment to paying them drove me. Because I knew I had to pay them, I *couldn't* give up, even if I had wanted to.

The key to this strategy's success was my communication with the vendors. By communicating with my vendors and being honest about my situation, my company was saved from bankruptcy, my dream was still alive, and everyone was paid. It was a tremendous lesson in using straightforward communication to create a win-win result. I also knew one thing for certain. If I was going to have to go out of business, it wouldn't be without giving it my creative all. This was late May, early June of 1997.

***Seed of Success:*** *Admit your mistakes; take responsibility for your actions. Don't run away or try to hide the truth. Face it all head on. If you do this, people will respect you in ways you've never imagined. More than you know, everyone in your life is affected by your actions.*

When dealing with vendors and clients, pay attention to how they react; stay tuned in to their feelings. By doing this, you can listen and respond in ways that will allow interaction to grow. The ripple effect of sincere, straightforward communication in business will astound you.

## Refocus on Strengths to Avoid the Trap Doors of Trouble

The first thing I did to refocus my energy was to go back to my strengths. Once I started focusing on my strengths, it became clear to me pretty quickly that I wasn't very good at running a factory. It was equally clear that my abilities for marketing and promotion were extremely strong — and they had brought me this far in the pie business — so I decided to focus on these attributes and base my recovery plan on them.

***Slice of the Pi(e):*** *When you focus on your strengths, things start to fall into place. It doesn't happen overnight, but the most important thing you can do for yourself professionally is to keep going back to an honest assessment of your strengths and weaknesses. By doing so, you will be able to recognize the trap doors and refocus your energies in a positive direction.*

The knowledge that my recovery strategy would be centered on my strengths in marketing and promotion gave me a new sense of freedom. I knew I would be able to perform at a new level of success as long as I was focused on doing what I knew best.

Examining my predicament in this new light made for an easy decision. I would shut down the factory and find a co-packer or contract manufacturer to bake my pies. So on June 1, 1997, I closed my factory's doors for good. As I stood there, one of my long-time Pieteam members told me it was the saddest day of her life. I turned to her in disbelief. I felt freer than I had since starting the business in 1994. I had overcome the emotional devastation of being conned, I had managed to stay out of bankruptcy for the moment, and I was now focused on using my strengths to save my business. By assessing my choices and choosing actions and behaviors, I had just made a decision that would change the fate of my company. I just needed to find someone to bake my pies.

***Seed of Success:*** *Organize your plan. Make a list of your goals and estimate a time schedule to reach each point. Even if you do not always hit these deadlines, you will have taken a very important step in reaching each milestone toward achieving your dream.*

# Rounding up the Right Resources

The food business is full of co-packers, companies that will produce your product using your recipe and package it in your box. Some pie production companies, like many other food producers, have excess production capacity in their facilities. By doing contract manufacturing for companies like mine, co-packers can use this excess capacity to create additional revenue, and thereby spread their existing fixed costs. And they also can lower their per-unit costs. As a result, these companies are able to produce pies at a cost less than I could produce at my own factory — and that's who I was looking for.

After some research and calling around, I found a small, family-owned bakery that I thought might be just right. When I visited this company, I had not shipped a single pie in six months. Why would a co-packer want to get involved in a situation where there was no business and where they would have to produce a high-end, thaw-and-serve pie they had never before produced on their manufacturing line? Simple. I just convinced them. I told them that with my marketing skills and their baking expertise, the sky would be the limit for sales and profits. My positive attitude and confidence sold them on the idea.

***Core Value:*** *A positive attitude attracts attention, which can bring you success. With the right attitude, life balance, and the knowledge of how to move ahead, your dreams can become reality. Many times we forget that we have complete control over our own attitudes and actions. You always have a choice — choose to keep it positive.*

It also helped that I told the bakery I would only buy tractor-trailer loads of Gordon's Pies from them. Now for a little perspective, a tractor-trailer holds about 7,000 pies. Up to that point, the most I had ever shipped at one time was 480 pies.

I had never told a lie in business before, and I knew I had to find some way to make good on this outlandish promise. So, added to the pressure of paying my vendors, I had to exponentially increase consumer demand for my pies in order to keep my word to this co-packer. The good news is, fulfilling the second promise would more than take care of the first, and I had my creativity and talent for promotion on my side. But even so, how in the world was I going to increase the demand for my product that much during a single summer? Again, the answer was simple. I would ask for it.

***Slice of the Pi(e):*** *It's incredible what is available in this world if you figure out what you want and simply ask for it — and keep on asking until you get what you need. Try it. You'll be pleasantly surprised at the outcome.*

Gordon's Pies was considered a cottage business — a small, regionally based product from an even smaller, regionally based manufacturer. Despite my limited distribution, I had every confidence in my product. I had personally delivered pies, personally sampled pies in the grocery stores, and personally spoken with bakery and store managers across New England. I had touched hundreds of thousands of customers through my exposure in the media. I truly believed that a supermarket could sell as many Gordon's Pies as it was willing to put on its shelves. The challenge was to convince the corporate grocery store executives of that fact. If I could convince the grocers that they could sell more pies, they would, in turn, *buy* more pies from me, and then I would buy more pies from my co-packer. It seemed to be a very logical solution.

# Finding Your Turnaround Strategy

Up to the summer of 1997, Shaw's Supermarkets had been my biggest customer. Of course, biggest is all relative. While I was shipping 480 pies at a time to Shaw's, I was shipping 240 pies to the Hannaford Brothers supermarket chain in Scarborough, Maine. I had done everything from working on the apple-peeling machine to putting pies in the shipping boxes to driving the delivery truck to the warehouse. It was time to take my project to the next level. My mindset was one of complete survival.

Every single day I reminded myself that I had to sell more pies or have my vendors turn back into creditors, have to file for bankruptcy, lose my dream, my business — and probably my house — and have to start over completely. I reminded myself daily that I had taken in $75,000 from friends and family members, including my parents and my in-laws, who had invested in me. I had to find a way to succeed so I could pay my creditors what I owed them, and then to pay my investors double their money back as I had promised when I had accepted their investment. I made the decision that I would not fail.

*Core Value: Develop a mindset of complete survival. Identify what you need to do to survive — and thrive — and then make certain that every step, every action, every decision, every single day, flows toward your survival. Make the decision that you will not fail.*

Despite all that had happened to me, I never took my eye off the fact that it was my responsibility to see the project all the way through. Although I may have struck some people as eccentric because of my outlandish marketing, thanks to my parents, my values have always been completely grounded and old-fashioned. Even though I marketed my products and my company in very creative ways, I was always true to my core values.

I knew that in grocery stores where Gordon's Pies were actually being displayed, they sold as quickly as the shelves could be restocked by store personnel. I also believed that if all stores used the supermarket axiom "pile it high and watch it fly," I could overcome my financial predicament.

Unfortunately, at that time, my product didn't provide the standard profit margin to the grocers. They were accustomed to selling a pie under their own brand name that was much smaller than my big three-pound apple pie and was baked off in the grocery store. The grocers purchased these pies from large manufacturers and made a hefty margin to boot. Not only would the grocers make less money on each Gordon's Pie they sold, but I was also selling a new concept — a fully baked and *then* frozen pie — a thaw-and-sell pie. It was completely unlike anything they were used to dealing with.

In addition, a big, loud, wacky guy was promoting the product by going from store to store, like some kind of Pie Piper. These were not the usual trappings of supermarket success. I was only starting to learn that change comes slowly in any business, but especially in the food business. I am not patient by nature, and my survival instincts eliminated what little patience I had.

I was now desperate to increase sales of Gordon's Pies, so I called Phil Francis, the then-president of Shaw's Supermarkets, directly. Shaw's was a $2 billion company and the number two player in the New England market. I convinced Mr. Francis to meet with me for twenty minutes the next morning so that I could plead my case. Remember, I needed

Shaw's to order tractor-trailer loads to make good on my promise to the bakery co-packer. I brought an assistant bakery manager from one of the few Shaw's stores that carried Gordon's Pies to this meeting. This particular Shaw's wasn't just *selling* the product, this assistant manager had told me — they couldn't keep the product on the shelves, even in the middle of the summer! What was the reason for this unbelievable volume? Because this particular store believed so much in the Gordon's brand, the product was merchandised in large quantities. This assistant bakery manager from one of Mr. Francis's very own stores was my living, breathing testimonial. And Mr. Francis listened. From that day forward, Shaw's only ordered tractor-trailer loads of Gordon's Pies for their stores. My agreement with my co-packer was saved, and I was well on the way to paying my vendors. I just had to stay focused and keep on going. I am so thankful that I followed my instincts. I learned from this turn in the road that a vital key to success was to trust my instincts.

***Seed of Success:*** *Any time you are in a position where you need to convince someone, think about using a testimonial. The third-party nature of a testimonial provides instant credibility to the person you are attempting to convince of the marketability of your product or service.*

***Core Value:*** *Remember to go with your instincts and your heart — your intuitive understanding of your own true path. Grok your dream — and rock the world! Don't hold back!*

## When a Door Opens, Be Ready to Walk Through It

At exactly the same time my company's future was hanging in the balance, my little sister Lisa got married. Her friend, Pam Coleman, the New York City bankruptcy attorney who had helped me regain my perspective back in the spring, had left her large law practice in January 1997 to coach college softball. She was, as she told me, living the "Year of the Whim." So I asked her to join my company.

I see now that, once again, I was putting another principle of Infinite Persistence — take action — to work. At the time, however, I just knew that having Pam as a key player on my team would change the direction of my company. I told Pam I could pay her a "hamburger joint" salary, which I then couldn't really afford, and give her common stock in my company. She first refused my offer, but I could see the entrepreneurial spirit in her bubbling up like a geyser. By the end of the wedding weekend, she agreed to join the team.

*__Seed of Success:__ A special note here from the "School of Hard Knocks" about giving away stock in your company. When starting a small business, find a way — any way — to entice employees without promising or actually giving up any of your own* *stock. I don't begrudge Pam one share, but I did give stock to many people who no longer have anything to do with my company. Take care of your team, but keep as much of your own stock as you can.*

Finding the right people for my company was key. I recognized in Pam qualities that would propel my company toward success, and having her join my team changed the course of my company's history.

***Slice of the Pi(e):*** *When events coincide and your instincts tell you a door is open, act quickly. And don't take "no" for an answer.*

On September 2, I began my fall 1997 "Pie à la Road Tour across New England" on the 44-foot Piebus. Pam met me in Kingston, New York, at the Hannaford Brothers grocery store.

During this whole time of saving my business, Pam and I did a lot of reading to educate ourselves. In fact, it was she who found an article in *Inc.* magazine about a company with a photo hall of fame. This idea inspired one of our best early grassroots marketing ideas to promote enthusiasm. On the spot, we decided to buy a Polaroid camera and take two photos at every store we visited, with store personnel and me, dressed in my wild costume, in front of the Piebus. We would leave an autographed photo for them to display in their store and then we would display the second photo in the Piebus itself. To this day, when I meet store personnel in my travels, they always ask if their picture is still on the Piebus Wall of Fame. From the Shaw's Supermarket in Bangor, Maine, to the toll booth operator in Schenectady, New York, to Frank Purdue, we were surrounded by thousands of smiling faces in the pictures that adorn the Piebus ceiling and walls.

 ***Seed of Success:** Read constantly and on a regular basis — even if it is just for*

*a short while every day. Study anything that has to do with small business, and learn as much as you can on a wide variety of business and industry trends and subjects. If you train your mind to absorb the information you'll find in books, business magazines, and business sections of major newspapers, it will feed your imagination, your intuition, and your base of knowledge so that you'll never have to sweat about being up to speed when things start to happen quickly in your business or a related industry. And you never know where your next great idea may come from!*

The Pie à la Road Tour across New England consisted of visiting grocery stores, meeting store and bakery managers, and attempting to convince these folks to install handmade, freestanding Gordon's Pies display units. Except for Thanksgiving, apple pie doesn't usually show up on many shopping lists. By merchandising Gordon's Pies in the in-store bakery, my goal was to turn apple pie into an impulse item.

Colorful, freestanding display units were one way to achieve this goal. Another good way would have been to inundate customers with advertisements, jingles, and special promotions, so that awareness of the product would permeate their consciousness. Then, when customers saw the product on the grocery shelves, their prior awareness of the product would make them more inclined to purchase it on impulse.

But advertising costs money and I had none, so I opted for the display unit route, once again finding a creative way to save money while accomplishing my goals. It's funny, but looking back, I had so many skills that I later abandoned and, thankfully, eventually rediscovered, such as finding cost-saving solutions.

When I shut down the factory and began to outsource production, I was left with a very large inventory of durable, brown, corrugated cardboard pie boxes. Instead of spending money we didn't have on $500 display units, we designed a freestanding display unit fabricated from these leftover pie boxes. I employed local Londonderry moms to partially assemble these displays, and I finished the construction of the displays at store level with a hot glue gun. Each display held between twelve and eighteen pies, depending on the daring of the bakery manager. I believed this display unit would transform Gordon's Pies into an impulse item for grocery store customers — and I was right.

 ***Seed of Success:*** *Be resourceful. Use what you have to create what you need. If you have the budget and you need an advertising campaign, by all means, go for it. But if you need to build awareness on a shoestring budget, look at what you have, who you know, or how you can retool old resources for a new use.*

## Sometimes It's All About Acquiring the Right Real Estate

The next challenge I faced was to persuade the grocers to allow these large display units on their sales floors in the first place. Just because a vendor such as Gordon's Pies wants a display unit on the grocery store sales floor, a grocer does not have to say yes. Too many of such displays can clutter the sales floor and obstruct grocery carts. So grocery store floor space is a valuable commodity, because, like all other real estate, there is only so much to be had. "Real estate" in supermarkets also includes space on their in-store bakery shelves.

The corporate buyer at Hannaford Brothers supermarket chain in Scarborough, Maine, my second largest client at the time, told me that if I could convince an individual store manager of the merits of my Gordon's Pies display unit, the unit would be approved for display in that store. Talk about a sales challenge. These displays came to symbolize the life or death of Gordon's Pies. We visited every Hannaford Brothers store in New England and upstate New York to sell them on the idea of allowing Gordon's Pies display units on their floors. More often than not, we succeeded. We were a force of nature that couldn't be stopped. I was focused on survival, and Pam was living her entrepreneurial dream. And at the center of it all was my marketing and promotional chariot, the 44-foot, wildly decorated Piebus that captured the attention and imagination of everyone we encountered.

Shaw's Supermarkets were different than Hannaford Brothers. It was a much more centralized operation. Floor positioning was all approved at corporate headquarters in West Bridgewater, Massachusetts. Because I had the approval of Shaw's president, Phil Francis, demonstrated by his authorization of tractor-trailer orders that same fall, I was allowed to install a Gordon's display unit in every single Shaw's store. But I still visited each and every one of those stores at least once that fall.

## Create Reminders of the Special Connections You Make With Your Customers

Taking pictures of me as a Supermarket Superhero with store personnel was a great marketing tool. With a constant reminder of our visit left behind, the store personnel were sure to never forget us. And, if they never forgot us, they wouldn't forget about Gordon's Pies!

It was during this time that my personality/celebrity status grew, to even my surprise, out of my wild marketing strategies. As we entered each grocery store, Pam would start introducing me: "This is Gordon — of Gordon's Pies. He's the *president* of Gordon's Pies," and so on. Pretty soon, one or two people would stop to figure out who I was. Then a few more people would stop. Then we would have a small crowd. We had actually, and somewhat inadvertently, created a celebrity around my out-of-the-box marketing strategies to promote my pies.

I had always worn shorts regardless of the temperature, and on my head I wore a Dr. Seuss, Cat-in-the-Hat-type hat made of felt with apples sewn on it. As the celebrity component began to grow, we realized that my outfit was not enough of a costume. Gradually, my Gordon's Pie garb became a tall, multicolored hat with bells, matching patchwork shorts, a red fleece vest, Mardi Gras beads, sunglasses, and a harmonica — the wardrobe ensemble of a true Supermarket Superhero. I gave away hundreds of T-shirts, and when we discovered that people really loved my Mardi Gras beads, Pam found a source for them in New Orleans and I started giving away beads by the thousands! People loved them and I loved them, too — as yet another inexpensive marketing tool. When people looked at those beads, they automatically thought of Gordon's Pies.

I also added the phrase "Oooo-La-La!"® to my repertoire as an additional way of attracting attention. It's a fun word that sounds even more fun coming loudly from a 6-foot-9 giant in full Supermarket Superhero regalia. I would enter a grocery store, head straight for the public address system, and announce, "Greetings and salutations, and happy apple pie revelations! This is Gordon, of Gordon's Pies, the Oooo-La-La Pie!" This *definitely* got people's attention, and once I had captured their interest, they were mentally engaged in their awareness of the Gordon's Pies brand.

*Slice of the Pi(e):* Become a "Force of Nature" in your marketing. Get out there and do whatever you have to do to sell yourself and your product or service. This calls for endurance, tenacity, and tireless enthusiasm. This aspect of Infinite Persistence is what being a force of nature is all about. Be strong; stand your ground, persist, and endure.

## Feel the Power of Connecting With Your Brand

During the tour, I met many veteran grocers who had met Frank Purdue when he was just starting to promote his "branded" chicken. Like I have since discovered with grocery store fruit pies, the meat in a grocer's butcher shop wasn't branded until Frank Purdue came along with his own method of promotion. He managed to change grocers' minds about stocking his more expensive chicken by traveling to each and every store, meat market, and New York City bodega to tell them personally about of the virtues of his product. Clearly, he succeeded. Not since the charismatic Frank Purdue, I was often told, had the grocers seen the owner of a food company tour the supermarkets.

For us, it was grueling and inconvenient, especially on a rickety old school bus, and the folks at the more than 500 stores I visited that fall appreciated the effort I was making to promote my product. That's why they all wanted to be part of my Piebus Wall of Fame. Even then they could see the future success of my brand.

*Slice of the Pi(e): Following in the footsteps of others to find your success also lays the groundwork for the future success of others who will follow you.*

# Tell Your Story — The Truth Is Your Best Marketing Plan

My marketing program has always been based on my real story as it has continued to unfold. To carry this out, I used the pie box as my canvas on which to paint this picture. On it, I talked about my family and my dream of creating the Great American Dessert. During the fall of 1997, being on the Piebus and in New England grocery stores literally twenty-four hours a day, seven days a week, I turned my marketing program way up in what I called my "grassroots, groundswell" marketing campaign.

I continued to tell my story everywhere I went. At this point, I was telling the story of my near bank-ruptcy, and how the Pie à la Road Tour became my strategy for survival. Customers and store personnel loved hearing my story. Showing people who I really was and what I had been through on my journey was yet another key to my success. Instead of an impersonal advertising campaign, I was a real guy telling a real story, and my real story wasn't pretty, but it was the truth.

Despite my crazy costume, they could see and feel that I wasn't just some made-up character trying to sell a product. I was a guy pulling out all the stops in order to survive and save my company. My story also struck a chord with my New England customers because I was one of them. And people responded. They started buying Gordon's Pies.

In addition, the way I was telling my story and the response my efforts had generated got the attention of the news media, and I was featured in numerous articles and on television programs that fall. New Englanders saved my company! The additional exposure spread my real-life example of what happens when you never give up all over the region and beyond.

*Slice of the Pi(e): Tell your story. Let people know who you are and why you're there. By allowing people to know you and your story, they will be able to identify with you and feel your dream. This is yet another way of marketing your brand, your product or service, and, ultimately, your dream.*

By the end of fall 1997, I had sold $1 million worth of pies to my grocery store clients. Since each pie was generally seen and consumed by three to four people once my customer got it home, we figured that just about one million New Englanders learned about and tasted Gordon's Pies that fall. That number totally amazed me.

## Say What You'll Do — and Do What You Say

Selling that $1 million worth of pies was critical, because it meant I could go back to my vendors who had agreed to give me time to raise cash and structure a way to pay back what I owed them. And that's just what I did. I had promised my vendors that I would come back to them in January 1998 with a payment plan. Ahead of schedule, I phoned and visited each of them during the first week of December 1997. Of the seventy-two vendors to whom I owed a collective $400,000, seventy-one of them signed the settlement and forbearance agreement that Pam had drawn up. It was an unbelievable feeling. I had not run from my responsibilities, but instead had committed myself to paying my vendors back — and I had succeeded. I never had to file bankruptcy.

## Keep Communicating With Your Customers

Pam said it was the fastest work-out she had ever seen in her entire legal career, and that the key to its success was my communication. I had given my creditors realistic road signs as to what lay ahead, and when we arrived at those points, I did the same for the next stretch of road. My vendors always knew where they stood with me, no matter what. Communication and honesty bought me the time necessary to figure out a plan, put it into action, and find a way to pay everyone what I owed them.

My success during the fall of 1997 also taught me another valuable lesson. Throughout 1996, I had only sold $400,000 worth of pies. In four short months in 1997, I had sold $1 million worth of pies. I had proven to myself that focusing on my strengths had worked. Once I started dedicating my time to marketing and public relations instead of worrying about baking the pies, I experienced success I never could have imagined. Focusing on my strengths was the ticket to my piece of the pie.

# Make Obstacles Your Opportunities

Unfortunately, there was still a little more to it than that. While my hands weren't covered in flour anymore, I still had to keep close tabs on my manufacturing partner. And when quality problems arose that fall, I was confronted with customers who had less-than-perfect experiences with Gordon's Pies. But, I realized, even that presented a new opportunity.

Every person who complained that fall received a personalized note from me, together with a refund, plus a little something extra. Although it wasn't my fault anymore if the apples were too hard or the bottom crust too doughy, my name was still on the box. It has always been my goal to provide the best possible service to my pie-loving customers, and I am proud to say that I have always tried to treat my customers like family. This means that every customer phone call comes directly to my cell phone, and every e-mail comes directly to my desk — even today, when Gordon's Pies is a national product.

I invite customers from Boston to Biloxi to call me directly and give me their comments, good and bad. And they do. This tactic has resulted in some of the most wonderful conversations with my customers, and the goodwill value has been immeasurable.

***Seed of Success:*** *Conscientious follow-up and extraordinary customer service are keys to your continued success — and the immeasurable goodwill of your customers.*

# Balancing the Trappings of Success Through Continuous and Honest Assessment

Selling $1 million worth of Gordon's Pies in 1997 presented yet another challenge. For the first time in my career, I had some money in the bank. Would I remain frugal, always looking for the least expensive — and free if I can find it — way to accomplish my goals and spend below my means, or would I start spending up to my means and beyond?

Unfortunately, the answer was the latter. My spending didn't start out of control. It more or less grew that way as time went by. First came salary increases for my Pieteam members. Then I actually took a big salary for the first time ever. Next, I added more players to my Pieteam.

I spent big money on a luxury car to "reward" myself. I realize now (hindsight is 20-20, the old saying goes) that I should have heeded my frugal instincts and stood by my conservative upbringing. I thought at the time that a material thing like a car would bring me happiness. Ironically, I was neglecting my wife and family, my true source of happiness. I needed to find a way to create a new sense of balance in my life, but I was a long way from that realization.

The fall of 1997 was grueling, but it was a hugely successful financial selling season. While I had worried constantly about my company's survival and my manufacturing partner's abilities to consistently produce a quality product, somehow I was still in business. I had paid off all my vendors. I had proven that I could create and manage a successful brand in New England. Gordon's Pies was showing solid sales at Shaw's and Hannaford Brothers. And, like every ambitious businessperson, this success had whetted my appetite for even more sales. And more sales meant that I could fuel more spending. I realize now that this was the point at which I should have stopped to assess my behaviors and habits.

*Slice of the Pi(e): It is very easy to get out of balance at the critical juncture between struggle and success. The Infinite Persistence principle of constant and honest assessment can keep you out of this trap. Using honest assessment of behaviors and habits, you can rebalance your priorities and expectations of success as well as failure.*

## Be Creative, but Keep Your Pants On

In 1998, Stop & Shop Supermarket Co. was the largest supermarket chain in New England. Since Gordon's Pies was successful at the other major New England grocers, I decided it was time to pursue Stop & Shop as a client. I had initially presented Gordon's Pies to Stop & Shop when I first started the business in 1994. Stop & Shop is a very successful supermarket chain — and very conservative. The first time I visited the Stop & Shop bakery buyer, I stripped down from my fancy suit into my boxers and T-shirt and then put on a baker's outfit. My message was, "I'm no longer a Boston public relations guy; I'm a baker." No one at the Stop & Shop market appreciated my humor and I was asked to leave the building.

I would not be dissuaded by this experience, however. At the time, my primary *modus operandi* for securing a new grocery store account was to go as high in a company as I could get, preferably the president's office, to the person I usually considered a visionary. After my experience with Shaw's president, Phil Francis, I believed that if I could convince a supermarket president of the huge benefits and potential of my marketing program, he would explain it to the people in his organization and make the program work. Although I thought this tactic saved time and effort, I discovered that this maneuver permanently compromised my good relationships with the buyers later on, because I had gone over their heads.

It seems like such an easy lesson, but it was very hard, painful, and costly for me to learn. I discovered the importance of following the rules of hierarchy in order to achieve my goal.

In the spring of 1998, I finally arranged a meeting with a Stop & Shop senior vice president and his bakery buying department. At the end of the meeting,

Stop & Shop agreed to test Gordon's Pies in ten of its stores throughout New England. The test that started in April 1998 became a full-fledged account later that year. During the spring of 1998, I also landed BJ's Wholesale Club, a New England-based club store, as an account. My company's pie sales in 1998 went through the roof and reached the sky!

## With Infinite Persistence, the Pie Just Keeps Getting Bigger

In 1998, I added to my supermarket and club store exposure by hosting "Pie Parties." To do this I had an on-air radio contest to pick a winner who would then receive a motivational Pie Party at their office. Pam and I would drive the Piebus to the winning company's offices with disco music blaring and would host a lunchtime party with free pies and T-shirts. There I told my story of *never give up, no matter what,* and of overcoming adversity. It was a terrific way to promote Gordon's Pies and a huge success all around. Word spread like crazy, and soon companies and individuals alike were calling to invite me to host morale-raising Pie Parties. The Pie Parties turned out to be another way to gain public attention and promote my pies on another level. And now I clearly see that it was also the beginning of my work in promoting the concept of Infinite Persistence.

## See Time as Your Friend

Even with such a monster sales season, the fall of 1998 was only slightly less stressful than the previous year. I had not yet mastered the concept of time as my friend. I had always set a grueling pace for myself, pushing my body and my mind beyond all reasonable limits — and despite that, I always ran out of time. I never took time to rest, because I didn't believe I *had* the time to rest. I worked in a constant frenzy, often living on two or three hours of sleep per night.

I also relentlessly pushed my Pieteam, as I was pushing myself, both personally and professionally. This relentless pushing often created tumultuous relationships, which deteriorated more with each passing day. And, after another successful fall selling season, I was starting to get fat, literally and figuratively. I was losing control of my weight, my finances, my priorities, and myself.

## Sometimes More Is Better, Sometimes More Is Worse — and Sometimes More Is Just More

For so long, I believed that more was better. So I spent more money to impress people and to convince myself of my success. I ate more because a pie man should not be thin and fit. I spent more time at work so that I could make more money. Then the stark realization of the emptiness in my life all this "more" was creating hit me. I finally realized that I overdid everything because I didn't really feel good about myself.

Now before you start thinking that I'm getting all "self-help" on you, here's the disclaimer that makes this important to my story. I am first-born and have no problem admitting that I have been and can be very selfish and demanding. But I'm also willing to admit how much being completely selfish has cost me personally and professionally — and that it just doesn't make any sense.

I realized "more" is not necessarily better. There is only a certain amount of money I can spend to make myself happy. Once I hit that point, no amount of money I spend beyond that can make me any happier. It's the same with food and time at work. I finally learned that every action I take is the result of my conscious choice, whether it is spending money, eating, or working. This was an amazingly liberating discovery for me and one that affected every part of my life.

***Slice of the Pi(e):*** *Most of us have been at a holiday table and taken that extra bite of turkey, candied yams, or apple pie, even when we knew we wouldn't be any more satisfied by doing it. In fact, that extra bite usually puts us over the edge into complete misery. Now picture the last time you stayed late at the* *office or finished a project at 2:00 a.m. Did working beyond your capacity yield any lasting benefit to you, your project, or your company? Or what about that purchase you made solely to impress other people with your success, but brought you little, if any, real joy? There's nothing wrong with buying quality or luxury as long as you know **why** you're spending the money, and that what you're spending your money on creates joy.*

## Raising the Bar to New Heights

Once I believed that I had become a force in the New England pie world, I set my sights on national sales. I had been featured on CNN's "Business Unusual" with Lou Dobbs in the fall of 1998, and I had been included on Lou's list of Top Retail Trendsetters in early 1999.

In the food business, like most other businesses, trade shows are an important way to connect with potential clients. I wanted to increase both my respect and connections in the pie industry more than anything at the time, and the only way I could see that happening was through these trade shows. Through 1998, I had participated in regional New England food shows. Since I was riding high from my success in the fall of 1998 and had some available cash, I decided that in 1999, Gordon's Pies would have a presence on the national trade show scene. I registered not only for the New England Fresh Food Association trade show, but the Retail Bakery Association's national show in Minneapolis and the International Dairy Deli Bakery Association's show in New Orleans.

## Go Big or Go Home

I didn't just want to attend these shows, I wanted to *dominate* them. I wanted these shows to create a media blitz for my company and make Gordon's Pies a national brand. I wanted to put my pies on every table in the country.

To make this splash, I decided to use the Piebus as the centerpiece of my trade show display, with huge television monitors flanking it. The TVs would continuously loop a video I directed, called "PIE." It had music and store-visit footage with supermarket executives and customer testimonials. It was fun and it was good.

Because of the size of the Piebus, I had to pay for several expensive booth spaces to accommodate it at the trade shows. Pam and I drove the Piebus to each trade show location, and then I flew in my other key Pieteam members for each show. By then, the Pieteam had grown to include my part-time food technologist, whom I had convinced to also act as my chief financial officer; a local woman I had hired to be my public relations director; an office assistant; and a local mom who had built my Gordon's displays as my customer service manager. I had also hired two former supermarket bakery managers as my Supermarket Ambassadors. The Ambassadors' jobs were to continue the Piebus's mission of delivering our freestanding displays to supermarkets, troubleshoot any quality problems, and serve as my envoys at store level. I had every level covered to promote my brand of pies — and a lot of people working for me.

Of all the attendees and exhibitors at all these shows, it was Mrs. Smith's Bakeries that was most clearly on my radar screen. (Remember, my original goal was to ultimately sell my company to Mrs. Smith's Bakeries in seven years. By then five years had passed, and the clock was ticking.) It was at the Retail Bakery Association's national show in Minneapolis that I was able to make this first important contact in what would be the chain of events and connections that ultimately led to reaching my goal.

When I first met Stuart Newton at the New England regional trade shows, he was a marketing manager with Mrs. Smith's. And since I wanted Mrs. Smith's attention, I asked Stuart for a meeting during the Minneapolis show.

I knew Mrs. Smith's was trying to figure out how to boost their presence in the marketplace — and that they were experimenting with the thaw-and-sell concept. I knew that if I could get their attention, they would be interested in talking to me because I had developed a pie product that no other company had yet introduced — the thaw-and-sell pie they had been looking for.

Pam and I met with Stuart Newton and other Mrs. Smith's executives on board the Piebus, positioned smack in the middle of the Minneapolis Convention Center. I was certain they would immediately recognize what a powerful marketing program I had in place, and that they would then want to buy my company. I had the correct vision — but the wrong timing. Mrs. Smith's wasn't interested in buying my company at that time. I later learned that they had wanted to see what more I could do — and how I would continue to dig into the pie market with my innovative marketing strategies.

One person from that first meeting with Mrs. Smith's did remain interested in Gordon's Pies, however, and that was Stuart Newton. Over the next two years, I saw Stuart at various trade shows, or, more accurately, Stuart saw me. I could tell he appreciated my marketing strategies, and I realize now that he was collecting information and waiting for the right time.

My trade show venture was, therefore, a very expensive proposition. Hotels, food, and all incidentals added up fast — and big. These two shows cost approximately $40,000. At the time, however, I was unconcerned. My sales were growing exponentially, I was making great money, and somebody else was manufacturing my product. I had even outgrown my first manufacturer and was now with a second co-packer.

## Bigger Isn't Always Better

Although I did end up dominating the trade shows by being larger than life and drawing plenty of attention to Gordon's Pies and the Piebus, I also managed to intimidate and put off people in the bakery business who were accustomed to doing business in a much more subdued manner. This was not the kind of attention I had wanted. I had hoped to gain positive recognition for creating and developing my "grassroots, groundswell" marketing campaign. Like a musical group, I had wanted to be "discovered," but the hard lesson I learned during my trade show domination was that the food business does not work like that.

On top of the trade show expenses, I also decided to run a radio advertising campaign in New England. I contacted a friend who was a media planner, instructed her to get the best deals possible, and turned her loose with a budget of $100,000. For that investment, I did get a nice radio campaign, and I did touch lots of customers.

While I really couldn't afford to continue the radio campaign for long, I certainly did make the most of the opportunity while it lasted. I taped a series of live interview spots with Pam asking me questions to which I would give unrehearsed, informal answers. These spots sounded great. I would then personally deliver these radio spots to the Boston-based radio stations in order to build goodwill and meet some of the on-air personalities.

*Seed of Success: If you ever run a radio advertising campaign, make sure you ask your account executive for live interviews. This option is rarely used. It was perfect for me.*

Once I had made a personal contact with a radio station, I would pull up to the studio in the Piebus and deliver warm pie to the disc jockeys just before morning and afternoon peak traffic times. I would then get to be on-air with the DJs during the all-important morning and afternoon drive times when everyone would be listening to their favorite radio station. In combination with the ads themselves, this exposure was awesome.

## Diet, Exercise, and Other Infinite Persistence Training Grounds

As I spent money with little or no control, I also lost control of my eating. Because I'm tall, I can carry a great deal of weight. But because of stress and lack of discipline, I started to pack it on heavily. My fighting weight is 215; I was up to 265 and didn't care. I was in the pie business, I told myself. I reassured myself that I shouldn't be thin. In reality, it was so unhealthy, but at the time I could rationalize anything for any reason.

For me, talking about weight is only slightly easier than talking about money. In the summer of 1999, I decided to lose those extra 50 pounds through a diet and exercise plan — and a few simple decisions I had to practice making over and over again, each and every day, until they became habits. My weight loss didn't happen overnight — in fact, it took me nearly a year — and that was terribly hard, especially for someone who is accustomed to instant gratification. But I lost the 50 pounds, and at 40 years old, I am now in the best shape of my life. If you make the decision to lose some weight, first, it is absolutely essential that you recognize that it probably took several years to gain the extra weight. Therefore, do not expect to lose it overnight.

So what does Infinite Persistence have to do with diet and exercise? Everything. Infinite Persistence is about finding your balance, taking one step at a time to realize your goals, and *never, never giving up, no matter what.* What better way to learn the magic of this concept than trying it out on these fundamental issues we can all relate to?

## Creating Infinite Persistence in Your Diet

Eat less. That's it. I told you I was all about keeping it simple. Improve the quality of the food you eat as much as you can, whenever you can. (We all know what that means.) Don't deprive yourself, eat a wide variety of healthy foods, and cut back on the *amount* of food you consume. Every time.

One of the best pieces of advice I've ever received on food choices came from Pam, who taught me to ask myself before I eat something less-than-healthy, "Is it worth it?" Sometimes a piece of homemade chocolate cake *is* worth it, but usually candy from a gas station store is not. The difference is making conscious choices about the food you consume. Try making it a habit to incorporate this question into your diet and see what a difference it makes.

I also started drinking a minimum of eight glasses of water a day. I'm convinced that without changing anything else in their diet, most people can lose weight just by increasing their water intake. Soda or coffee or seltzer doesn't count. It has to be eight glasses of noncarbonated water every day.

*Slice of the Pi(e): Instill discipline. And the way you take care of yourself is a good place to start. Make sure that every decision you make in your life is a result of your conscious choice. Align these choices with the goals you have set in all the areas you have chosen to focus on, and constantly evaluate your decisions in order to make sure you stay on track.*

# Infinite Persistence in Exercise

Make a commitment to exercise at least ten minutes a day. That's it — just ten minutes a day. You know what exercises you enjoy, so choose any combination of those. You also know what intensity is comfortable and healthy for you, so do that. This is so much simpler than most people try to make it. Lose the all-or-nothing thinking and just do something for ten minutes a day, every day, and see what a difference it makes over time. Once you start with ten minutes a day, at some point you'll probably want to keep going after the initial ten minutes. But don't worry about that yet. The critical part is to commit to exercising ten minutes each and every day.

*Slice of the Pi(e): We have a gigantic industry built around making all this basic diet and exercise wisdom very complicated and mysterious. If you enjoy all that drama, go for it. But it truly is as simple as eating less, making better food choices, exercising, and* *drinking more water. Every day, one step at a time, until you reach your goal. And **never give up, no matter what**.*

Partially from all the hours spent riding in the Piebus and living on the road, I required back surgery. Following this surgery, I was only out of the office one day — against my doctor's recommendation — and at the time, I was *proud* of that fact. I know now that was me just not being able to let go, even for a day. It also showed me that learning balance in matters pertaining to my physical health was a challenge that I needed to address for my sake and the sake — and success — of my company. In learning the lessons of Infinite Persistence on the smaller, personal scale, I began to develop the awareness and insight that would prepare me for the bigger stuff ahead.

# Infinite Persistence in the Circle of Relationships

The lessons of Infinite Persistence kept building, blending one into another to create my deepening understanding of how this amazing and powerful force works to improve every single area of life. During the time I was so terribly out of balance with my weight, my timing, and my finances, I was also in a terrible way with my wife, Cindy. We fought constantly and were on the verge of divorce, because I also had lost sight of what was most important in my life — my family.

It was 1999, and in addition to the weight issue, spending money like crazy, and being seriously at odds with my wife, I began to notice that all the other relationships around me were deteriorating as well. This included troubles with my partner, Pam, my food technologist, and most of my grocery store clients — because I did not believe that any of them fully appreciated what I brought to the mix. I was still driving my luxury car, and I had doubled my salary draw to pay for all my excess. Then I lost my first customer, BJ's Wholesale Club. This was a rude awakening for me, but I now recognize it as the lesson of realistic expectations.

## Using Infinite Persistence to Keep Your Expectations Realistic — And to Know When to Let Go

The delicate balance of Infinite Persistence lies in the grey area between aiming for the sky and keeping your feet on solid ground. This is very easy to say and extremely hard to do. In the process of making yourself do or be anything you want to if you just pursue it with all your heart and never give up, it is easy to lose sight of what is realistic and what is not. Realistic expectations are double-edged swords, and I have been cut by both sides. On the one hand, if you limit your expectations in the name of being realistic, you may shortchange yourself of achieving more than you think you can. On the other hand, to stubbornly forge ahead on something that is unwise, unhealthy, or truly not possible is extremely detrimental to your ultimate result.

This is really where you have to learn to listen to your intuition and let your inner guidance system help you know when to stop moving down a particular path and find a new route to your ultimate destination. For example, I fully expected the Wonka-esque pie factory to be the ticket to my success — and after a time, it was clearly apparent that I had to let it go and create a different set of expectations.

***Slice of the Pi(e):** While setting goals, making plans, and taking the action steps along the timeline you create are key to making things happen, often it is knowing when to let go of ideas, goals, people, and expectations that holds the secret to pursuing your dreams with complete openness to possibility. To achieve the kind of clarity that allows you to "hear" the soft voice of intuition clearly demands the balance we've been talking about — the physical, mental, and emotional equilibrium that invites your intuition to help you see your path, including its inevitable twists, turns, and detours, clearly.*

When it comes to unrealistic expectations, it is possible that Gordon's Applesauce tops them all. As we were preparing our sales projections for 1999 — that year of excess, lost perspective, and important lessons in Infinite Persistence I only now appreciate — we decided to start marketing a new product, Gordon's Applesauce. We had a great relationship with our apple supplier, and the product was fabulous. Although we knew that Mott's dominated the category, we thought that with our brand recognition in New England, there was plenty of room in the applesauce business. We were mistaken in this assumption, and we seriously overprojected our sales numbers to set goals we could never achieve.

But before I accepted that important reality, I went out and sold the applesauce to our current clients. I sold it hard, never taking no for an answer, even when "no" was the answer sincerely given. I wasn't listening to my customers, and this laid the groundwork for my rude awakening.

**Core Value:** *Train yourself to truly listen when someone else speaks. This key skill provides the ability to understand and communicate clearly the messages from others that you need to hear.*

I went to BJ's Wholesale Club first with my applesauce, since the senior people there had always liked my personal appearances. BJ's put me in touch with their applesauce buyers, who informed me that without a solid sales base for the product, it was not going to sell well in their discount club setting. They were right, but I didn't like the way they delivered their message. So I went right to the top — right over everyone's heads, including my supporters. My imbalanced thinking prompted this huge error in judgment, and due to my rash behavior, BJ's ended up canceling their entire Gordon's order, pies included. This huge loss was what it took to open my eyes to my extreme imbalance. I realized then that my behavior and my habits were out of control. Finally, I knew it was time for a change. I apologized to everyone involved at BJ's and continued to pursue other sales avenues.

*Slice of the Pi(e): Keep your emotions and reactions balanced. Staying on an "even keel" will allow you to view situations and challenges with an open mind and heart. If you are on an emotional high, you will not see the whole picture. And if you allow your-self to become trapped in a low point, you cannot see the infinite possibilities.*

## Know That Your Mistakes Are Always Part of the Bigger Plan

Eventually, my Gordon's Applesauce did perform nicely and achieved a loyal following. I decided to "give" the Gordon's Applesauce program to my children Emily, 9, and Jack, 6, to manage. Since I didn't plan on having a physical shop to pass on to them, I gave them this opportunity early in their lives to experience the business world firsthand. As owners, they attend meetings concerning their product at supermarket corporate offices, they help develop marketing and promotional ideas with me, and they even have business cards!

But the roller-coaster ride of 1999 didn't end with just losing BJ's. My tumultuous relationship with my food technologist-turned-chief-financial-officer also came to a head. I had tried to turn this kind gentleman, who was an excellent food technologist and food cost accountant, into a CFO. In doing this, I had not only tried to put a square peg in a round hole, but then I tried to force that peg to fit the hole. In the spring of 1999, he resigned.

This huge loss taught me that it was critical to allow other people to focus on their true strengths, not just my own perceptions of what they should do or be. I had already learned that lesson when it came to focusing on *my* key skills for the best results, so now I got to revisit the same lesson as it applied to the Pieteam.

I was at a critical juncture, but I still wasn't ready to learn the financial lesson life was trying to teach me. Instead of using this loss as an opportunity to finally take hold of my own financial reins, I decided once again that I needed someone else to run the finances and back-room operations of Gordon's

Pies. I wanted to concentrate only on marketing and public relations — the more "creative" aspects of my business. What I hadn't yet accepted was that *all* of business is creative — it's just a matter of perspective. I was beginning to realize that everything was related to perspective. It affected how I viewed things, which in turn dictated my behavior and my reactions.

## Change Your Perspective, Change Your Reality

At the time, I told myself that what I really needed was a "real" chief financial officer, so I hired a CFO with a great deal of experience in corporate America. When my new CFO came on board, she analyzed where the company stood financially, and it wasn't a pretty picture. She also reviewed and analyzed the responsibilities that all my Pieteam members were handling at the time.

It turned out that I had members on the Pieteam I couldn't afford who were performing tasks already being performed by someone else in the company. We tried to find ways around the inevitable, but we couldn't. I had to let some people go. This was very sad, because I had only asked people to join the Pieteam whom I liked and trusted and who had vision for the project and believed in my dream.

I also realized that I didn't need a CFO with that much high-level experience; I needed to be the one to take control of my finances, and nobody could do that but me. I had pushed myself through so many tough challenges already, but the simple truth was that I was intimidated by my company's finances. I shouldn't have been, but I was. Once I realized what I needed to do in order to take charge of my company's finances, I found that with a little effort, everything was fairly easily figured out. The hardest part was just facing what needed to be taken care of.

**Core Value:** *Accept change as a partner. Remember that life is a constantly changing experience. When you treat problems as opportunities, it can open the door to positive change in your life.*

# Finding the Break in the Clouds

I ended the tumultuous year 1999 with a new CFO, fewer Pieteam members, one less grocery store client, and many rocky relationships all around me due to what I perceived as a collective lack of vision. My third manufacturer — and the owner of my last co-packer — had just shut its factory's doors after seventy-five years of baking.

But there were some bright spots. I was continuing to build the Gordon's brand in New England. My Pie Party program was growing, and I was starting to tell my "pie story" in speeches I was giving all over New England, to audiences that included many business-school students.

Also that fall, Cindy gave birth to our third child, Sam. It pains me to admit it, but I was so consumed with work that I was on my cell phone in the hospital right after Sam's birth. Even for major life events, I didn't allow myself the time to breathe. I am so blessed that Cindy is such a wonderful and forgiving person. She tells me now that she loved me not only for the person I was, but for the person she knew I could grow to be. I now thank my lucky stars for her every day, and she truly is my pie angel.

**Core Value:** *You have to live with your decisions and your actions. Keep both of these things aligned with your priorities. Don't yield to the external pressures — always search your heart and your instincts and do what is right for you. Not everyone may like it, but you will feel good about the person looking back at you in the mirror. You will feel it in your heart.*

## Remain Open: Education Is Everywhere

The speeches to business-school classes were great opportunities for me to tell my story. Often, the ideas and advice I received from these sophisticated audiences were very enlightening. I remember two entrepreneurial classes in particular, one at Babson College and one at Bentley College, where the students were really on the ball. Their suggestions as to how to expand the Gordon's brand both in and out of New England infused me with the breath of fresh air I so badly needed.

***Seed of Success:*** *Sometimes all it takes is the sincere input from a bright, fresh young mind to reignite a dulled imagination. The next time you need to solve a work-related problem, ask someone with no experience whatsoever. In fact, ask a child. You'll be surprised at the clarity of their perspective. Kids don't see the complications. They focus on the simplicity of a situation. Without focusing on the obstacles, they see solutions clearly.*

***Slice of the Pi(e):*** *Be creative in your problem solving. Remember that every problem is an opportunity for positive change — and a fresh jump into the world of infinite potential.*

# The Power of Fun — A Publicity Tip

On Valentine's Day 2000, I reaffirmed for myself the power of fun. Dressed as a 6-foot, 9-inch Cupid Pie-Dude, complete with red tights, wings, and a giant bow and arrow, I helped a young couple reaffirm their marriage vows on the Boston Commons. Instead of a wedding cake, we provided a three-tiered Gordon's Apple Wedding Pie. Not only was it fun, despite the 15-degree weather, but this glorious stunt landed us on the front page of *The Boston Globe*. Just imagine *that* as proof of what you can accomplish when you engage your most flamboyant creativity!

# New Hats, New Creativity

In 2000, in addition to her other responsibilities as my business manager, Pam also took on the job of salesperson. We realized that without new sales, there was no way to continue to grow the business. I had to be able to pay my remaining Pieteam members and hit our aggressive sales goals.

Pam drove to New York City, then to Washington, D.C., and back every few weeks to meet with potential clients. It was a hard sell, too, because while the profit margin we could offer grocers was now a little better using a co-packer, it still wasn't the profit they were used to. To compound this challenge, I didn't yet have any presence in either the New York or Baltimore/Washington markets. So Pam's creativity kicked in. She convinced some of these grocers to *test* Gordon's Pies in their stores — and a few others to carry our product outright. Then we launched our product with Metro Foods of Baltimore by taking the Piebus on a Metro store tour with the Metro bakery buyer and Metro's president on board.

This store tour was a first in supermarket history, and we capped off this day of continuous store visits and media coverage with a huge pie giveaway in front of the Hard Rock Café at Baltimore's Inner Harbor.

But despite my Pieteam's collective efforts to expand our territory into these areas, we ran into obstacle after obstacle. I knew something was still not quite right, but I also sensed that change was on the way.

***Seed of Success:*** *Stay in touch with the people in the business situations you encounter. Be personable and respectful and reach out to your vendors, customers, and clients as human beings just like you. By doing this, you will be able to temper your own behavior and react in ways that will allow positive relationships to grow.*

## Take a Break to Invite a Shift in Perspective

In March 2000, I took a three-day vacation that literally changed the course of my life, both personally and professionally. On that vacation, I read *The Millionaire Next Door* by Ph.D.s Thomas J. Stanley and William D. Danko. The insights I gained were incredible, and they significantly affected my view of my financial situation. I made a decision then and there that I would change my financially irresponsible ways. I would stop my uncontrolled spending, begin saving, and take active steps to increase my net worth or, as the authors describe it, become a "prodigious accumulator of wealth." When I make up my mind about something, I am very disciplined to incorporate the appropriate concepts. These authors provided the concepts I was finally willing to live by.

***Seed of Success:*** *Learn about your finances. Pay attention to your budget, on both personal and business levels. Don't work your life away believing you have to wait for retirement to accomplish your financial goals. You can make them come true now. Buy a book, talk to a friend, meet with an accountant. Ask questions and get direction. This will help you focus on financing your dream.*

The first thing I did when I came back from this insightful vacation was to sell my luxury car and start driving the company's fully paid-for, painted-up Jeep Wrangler, affectionately referred to as the

Piejeep, which was also a rolling billboard for Gordon's Pies. Next, I made an appointment with my accountant to fully explore my financial health, I hired a lawyer to prepare wills and trusts for Cindy and the kids, I updated my life insurance policies, and I essentially laid the foundation for improving my overall personal financial health. I needed to be accountable and aware of our spending — to actually begin tracking where the money was going.

## Make Continuous and (Brutally) Honest Assessments

That spring and summer, I took a serious inventory of my personal finances. I also read *Your Money or Your Life* by Joe Dominguez and Vicki Robin, which further challenged me to evaluate my spending habits. I learned to have more confidence in my financial decisions, especially when they weren't glamorous or impressive. I found that all money transactions were important, even the small ones.

But the biggest lesson I learned — one I hope I can

pass on to you — was the importance of being brutally honest with myself about money. How much did I really need? How much did I spend just for appearance? How much did I need for my family's future, and how much of that had I already saved?

These are not easy questions to ask or answer, but I urge you to take this exercise and do it for yourself. It makes all the difference in the world. And don't attempt this task alone. Ask your accountant for advice, and if you don't have an accountant, ask someone whose financial wisdom you trust. But start today. Once my personal finances were in order, I was able to bring the same financial grounding to my business.

*Core Value: Hope is the ingredient that can get you through the days when the sun doesn't shine and propel you through the challenges that come your way.*

One way to accomplish the financial grounding I needed in my business, I decided, was to start giving back to my community as a token of my appreciation for all of my blessings and accomplishments. At my mom's recommendation, I became a national spokesman for the National Mentoring Partnership to raise awareness of the critical need for mentors for kids across the country.

**Core Value:** *Share your success. Find a way to share it with others by contributing to something that is important to you. Touch the lives of others and you will be truly successful beyond all financial and personal gain — you will have made a difference in the world. This is the ultimate level of success in any endeavor.*

In conjunction with my Gordon's Support Kids Mentoring Campaign, I developed *Gordon's Be Everything You Want to Be* coloring and activity book, designed to make kids feel good about themselves while learning the children's version of the Gordon's Pies story. I handed out thousands of these books all over New England. If you're ever feeling down and want to feel good about yourself, give positive and educational stuff away to kids and spend a little time talking to them. Seeing children's faces light up like it's their birthday is an incredible experience — and one in which you truly receive as much as you give.

## Take Time to Take Stock

Then, in the summer of 2000, I did something that, at the time, was criticized by everyone from my parents to my children. I took the entire summer off. On June 1, 2000, I took Pam and my CFO out to breakfast and told them that, effective that day, I was on sabbatical for three months. I needed a break from the day-to-day pressures of running my pie business in order to fully sort out what I wanted and needed for my company's future. I spent that entire summer with Cindy and the kids at our weekend home in

Sunapee, New Hampshire, which I nicknamed the "SSP," for Special, Special Place. There, I became a husband and a dad again and gently allowed my mind to wrap itself around all the concepts and ideas that were important about my company. Trusting my intuition, and giving myself the space and time I needed to listen and reflect, allowed me to gather my thoughts and refuel for the many challenges to come.

***Seed of Success:** Everything related to your performance is important, and your efforts to organize and prioritize your time are imperative to the realization of your dream. Prioritize your time, every single day, both on personal and on business levels. Decide what is most important to you in your life and make those things your most important daily focus. And be realistic. You can't do everything — and if you try, you may undermine the very success you're overextending yourself to achieve.*

# Keep Refocusing on Your Strengths

One thing I knew for sure about myself was that I had a gift when it came to marketing. My instincts and impulses were always right on the money about finding new and exciting ways to reach my customers. Upon reflection, it became crystal clear to me that I was still too busy worrying about manufacturing, distribution and sales calls to concentrate on my key strength — marketing. I made some terribly hard decisions that summer and early fall when I returned to the office and to the 2000 Pie à la Road Tour. During my time off, I had come up with a plan that I thought would take my company even further on the road to success. The idea was to reinvent Gordon's Pies as a much smaller operation, and Pam and I focused completely on marketing and public relations. She balked, but I knew it was the right path, so I trusted that her instincts would turn her around, and that my own would keep us moving forward with this new idea.

# Make the Hard Choices and Keep Moving Forward

My first project when I returned from sabbatical was to find new offices for Gordon's Pies. I needed new surroundings for the changes my new plan would bring — and to help create yet another new perspective. We moved into the new space in late September of 2000, and on October 10, Gordon's Pies became a two-person marketing and promotion company. While the concept seemed simple, executing it was anything but that. In order for the company to survive, I had to cut down to the basics, and the answer was as simple as pie. I had to let people go. I agonized over how to tell my Pieteam members, and then I decided to just jump in and tell them. It was one of the hardest things I have ever done, but it was necessary in order to continue on the new path I had chosen for my company.

 **Core Value:** *Faith is a level of infinite confidence that is hard to define. It must*

*come from within your heart and be spurred on by your belief. Draw upon it to attain your dreams.*

Figuring out this new model for my company to follow didn't solve all my problems, of course. I still had manufacturing issues to resolve. Quality concerns were still rampant, and delivery happened on a wing and a prayer, but I felt freer than I had since I started the company. My life had become an adventure again. I realized that I didn't need to have lots of employees to have a "successful" business. I just needed to have a good idea that I believed in, a small staff that was as passionate as I was, and confidence in myself that, no matter what, I could and would find solutions to all the challenges that showed up to teach me what I needed to know. I now realize that in committing myself to facing these challenges, I placed my feet firmly on the path to understanding the concept I now recognize as Infinite Persistence.

*__Seed of Success:__ The power of people working together with Infinite Persistence cannot be underestimated. Teamwork, networking, and partnerships create systems that will allow you to forge ahead through the challenges. Be a master of systems to increase your efficiency and do more in less time. To do this, create a network of key people with the skill sets you need, then build a system for the most efficient accomplishment of each task in your master plan. You may experience some trial and error, but once you achieve this "network of success," you will have an ideal system, tailored to your business's unique needs. Be creative!*

In October 2000, I met Linda Patton, also in Mrs. Smith's marketing department, at a trade show in Atlantic City. Linda instantly showed her appreciation for my marketing abilities, and she became a big supporter of Gordon's Pies back at Mrs. Smith's. Her support and endorsement gave me even more presence at Mrs. Smith's and moved me further along the path to my goal.

Then the biggest break of my career came later during that fall of 2000. Earlier that summer, Pam had completed the lengthy paperwork necessary to become an official supplier in the Wal-Mart distribution system. This was not an easy task, even for Pam the lawyer! But all that paperwork paid off a few short months later when the Wal-Mart buyer ordered two tractor-trailer loads of Gordon's Pies for sale in the New England market during the Thanksgiving and Christmas holidays.

Wal-Mart puts a tremendous value on what I refer to as "retailtainment." Retailtainment is anything at store level that gets customers and store associates excited about buying and selling merchandise. To this end, the folks at Wal-Mart were extremely interested in having me do personal appearances in my King Gordon of Pie get-up in their stores.

And my Gordon's Pie Parties were also perfect for the Wal-Mart customers. When I was in their stores doing my King Gordon shtick, the air of excitement and fun was palpable, and the customers were soon buzzing about the possibilities of hosting a Gordon's

Pie Party at their places of business, churches, and schools. Wal-Mart customers also loved to try — and then buy — Gordon's Pies during these appearances. Store associates felt special that I was visiting their stores. All in all, it was a match made in merchandising heaven.

As the details were being finalized and appearances scheduled, Pam reminded me that when we first started the Pie à la Road Tour, she often had to *beg* grocery store managers for permission for me to appear in costume in their stores — and suddenly we had a waiting list! Our creative marketing had definitely paid off.

***Seed of Success:*** *Establish credibility and then back it up by exceeding the expectations of your clients or customers. Do this by delivering a superior service or product, one customer at a time, time after time. With this kind of credibility, your market niche will grow steadily, and your business will continue to thrive.*

Of course, the fiscal — and physical — challenges during all this marketing excitement were real and concrete. I owed my co-packer more than $300,000. No plan had been put in place to pay back my investors, whom I had promised a doubling of their investment. Various vendors had been put on sixty- to ninety-day terms by my accounting staff, and I broke my hip on the first day of the 2000 ski season, forcing me to spend the next ten weeks on crutches. But regardless of the challenges, I had just shipped my first tractor-trailer load of pies to Wal-Mart.

In January 2001, we moved the whole Gordon's Pies operation to my house, back where it all began. I had since built an addition onto my house before my son, Sam, was born. This addition included a nursery for Sam and an office for me. Pam and I moved our offices into this space in late January, while I was still on crutches recovering from my ski accident. With total focus on what had to be done, there was no time to think about my injury.

# In Dark Times, Keep Your Focus on the Bright Spots

Although the challenges of late 2000 were formidable, the Wal-Mart order had given us a definite sense that nothing could stop us. And, with the help of my accountant and his incredible team, Pam and I became our own bookkeepers, learning about our financial condition from the ground up. While it wasn't a pretty picture, we saw it up close, in person, with no disclaimers or excuses.

For the second time in my company's history, we put together a payment plan for all of our debt, including the repayment of my investors, and this time we eventually accomplished it all. One of my proudest days in business was the day I wrote checks to the eleven friends and family members, including my parents and in-laws, who had invested in me back in 1994. These believers not only doubled their money, but they also got to see that believing in a dream is worth the risk of investment.

***Seed of Success:*** *Be willing to take risks in order to obtain the big rewards. Do your homework, ask your questions, use your instincts, and then reach as high as you can — the reward will be worth the effort.*

## Learn the Language of Numbers

I managed to make these dramatic changes to my deplorable financial situation by simply facing the truth. My CFO had a great phrase, "the numbers always tell the story." I never really understood what that meant until I actually looked at my own numbers. Let's face it, most of us have never been taught how to really look at our business numbers; it's intimidating, and we think that's our accountant's job. Unfortunately, it sometimes takes something dramatic to convince people to open their eyes to the story the numbers are telling about their business.

***Seed of Success:*** *Learn the story your numbers have to tell now, before you have to scramble. Look closely at where you spend your money, at how much debt you have, and at your future financial obligations, both business and personal. These events are not going away, no matter how much you ignore them. Meet these future challenges head on, on your terms rather than theirs.*

## Start Today

The best advice I can give you with regard to getting your financial house in order is to start today. Don't wait another moment. It doesn't matter that you've spent the last twenty years hoping you'll have enough money when the need arises. You can start reversing the ill consequences that kind of financial planning will bring by taking the first step today. I know, because I did it. Except for my low-interest mortgages, I am now personally debt-free. It is an incredible feeling to know that you have faced this challenge head on and triumphed. But even though financial recovery doesn't happen overnight, if you start planning today and keep persisting, no matter what, each day will bring you closer to your eventual financial freedom. It's all about choice, commitment, and Infinite Persistence.

After receiving that first big Wal-Mart order in the fall of 2000, I had scheduled a meeting with the Wal-Mart buying office to review the Gordon's Pie program with them. So on May 1, 2001, I attended the biggest meeting of my career in Bentonville, Arkansas, at Wal-Mart's home office. I kid you not when I say that it felt like going home.

I had read Sam Walton's book, *Made in America: My Story*, when I first started my company, and I had reread it in 2000 when I had my financial epiphany. To walk the same streets Mr. Walton had, and to visit the town where he had started the largest company in the world, was an incredible experience for me. Even now, after having been to Bentonville scores of times, I still get goose bumps. For me, it's a magical, magical place — not unlike Disneyland — a place where dreams came true. The story of Wal-Mart is a source of inspiration to all the believers and dreamers out there, and it illustrates how perfectly Infinite Persistence works in a business setting.

Pam and I were never so prepared for a meeting in our lives. We talked to everyone we could find with knowledge of Wal-Mart, we reread Walton's book, and we spoke to Wal-Mart bakery and store managers for feedback. In that May 1 meeting, the Wal-Mart buyer told us that my pie was good, our sales were decent, and our "retailtainment" model was amazing, but our markdowns were too high and our retail price point was also too high. ("Markdown" means a store has to sell a Gordon's Pie for less than the full retail price point if it doesn't sell for full price after four days.) "Fix these things," the Wal-Mart buyer told us, "and we'll let you test again."

Rather than feel any discouragement, I saw this as my chance to do business with Wal-Mart. I had my sights set on a national account, and I saw the way laid clearly before me. The Wal-Mart buyer reminded me more than once, however, that this was only a test.

After all the challenges I had already met, I was ready to face this test with all of my energy and ability to persist. I knew I would *never give up, no matter what.*

I was so excited and confident in my ability to reach customers that, in my mind, I was only a few short months away from having a national account. I truly believe that there is great power in saying something out loud, and when you can truly envision something happening, it will come true. I had wanted to establish a national brand since the day I started my company, so I kept saying it out loud. "The test will be successful, the test will be successful." Even without personal experience, I knew that in order to satisfy Wal-Mart's demands, Gordon's Pies would have to change course yet again.

# The Infinite Power of People Connections

I sensed that it was time to tap my connection with Mrs. Smith's for help in solving the challenges that lay between where Gordon's Pies stood then and a successful Wal-Mart test. To do this, I first contacted Stuart Newton to talk it over and see what he thought I should do to address the markdown and price point issues raised by the Wal-Mart buyer. Stuart went to work on this, and after several calls and a series of starts and stops, I was overjoyed to learn that Mrs. Smith's would be willing to manufacture Gordon's Pies for Wal-Mart. It hadn't hurt my cause that at that time Wal-Mart was poised to become the largest company in the world. Oooo-la-la! The Pie King was ready to roll!

In July and August, Pam and I met with Stuart Newton and then with Mark Courtney, Mrs. Smith's senior vice president of sales and marketing, to finalize the arrangements for Mrs. Smith's to manufacture Gordon's Pies. Not only did we solidify Mrs. Smith's participation on the Wal-Mart account, but at that time Mark also asked if we would be interested in selling Gordon's Pies to Mrs. Smith's. This was a dream come true — and one of my biggest goals since the beginning. With great excitement, we started negotiating our deal.

A story befitting the Mrs. Smith's and Gordon's Pies legend happened late that summer. While we were still in the process of negotiating, I thought it might help the folks at Mrs. Smith's to see firsthand an example of my "grassroots, groundswell" marketing tactics — and just how extremely creative I could be. After all, if they wanted to buy the Gordon's Pies brand, they should at least see what they were getting into.

At 3:00 o'clock one morning, Pam and I entered the campus of Mrs. Smith's beautiful and pristine corporate headquarters in Suwanee, Georgia. I had just been to a local Wal-Mart (where else?) and bought spray paint and two life-sized plastic deer. Pam and I taped together and then strung two bed sheets high above the gorgeous building. On the sheets I had spray-painted the message "Fall 2001 —

Hunting for Millions in Sales — Mrs. Smith's and Gordon's Pies." Then, I painted the two deer in camouflage with two huge bull's-eyes on them. We were just about to make our escape when Tony Crook, who heads up bakery sales at Mrs. Smith's, caught us red-handed. I had never been caught pulling a prank before. To his credit, Tony just laughed and went in to work. He still ribs me about it every time we see each other, but as goofy as it was, it *did* get Mrs. Smith's attention! Getting people's attention, after all, was one of my innate strengths that has propelled me to success, time and time again.

Throughout our negotiations with Mrs. Smith's, Mark Courtney showed an incredible vision for the program and was extremely savvy in his dealings with us. I appreciated the experience all the way through.

*Slice of the Pi(e): Negotiate your way to success. Learning how to negotiate is crucial to your success, but it's not that hard. Connect with the people, listen to your instincts, do your homework, and rely on the knowledge you have gained from your experiences. Be persistent; do not step away from the challenge of a tough negotiation. Have no fear and know that you can get what you want — so be willing to walk away and try again another day. Trust that if you persist with integrity, the right deal will come together in a win-win solution for everyone. When the right ingredients of a sweet deal come together at the right time, negotiation can be as easy as pie!*

## Everyone You Meet Is a Player in Your Life and Dreams

On September 7, 2001 — six years and ten months ahead of my goal — we signed a Letter of Intent to sell Gordon's Pies to Mrs. Smith's Bakeries. And by early October, I had realized my pie-in-the-sky dream: Gordon's Pies had at last achieved a national distribution to all Wal-Mart Supercenters — more than 1,000 stores nationwide.

A week before we signed the contract, I had the immense good fortune to be featured on the CBS "Early Show," CNBC "Squawk Box," and the NBC "Early Today Show" on National Pie Day. An amazing southern gentleman named Billy Bob Bryson, who worked for Mrs. Smith's and played the guitar like nobody's business, made that experience all the richer by flying in from Arkansas to New York City for these appearances. Billy Bob accompanied me on television and played my theme song, "EAT MO' PIE!" People from all over the world telephoned and e-mailed me to ask where they could buy a Gordon's Pie — and where could they could get a recording of "EAT MO' PIE!"

## There's Always a Bigger Perspective to Consider

But in the middle of all this Wal-Mart excitement for Gordon's Pies, the unbelievable tragedies of September 11 rocked the security of people all over the world. That morning, Pam and I flew out of Manchester, New Hampshire, on our way to

Washington, D.C., where we were to meet with the executive director of the National Mentoring Partnership to discuss my new relationship with Wal-Mart and the opportunities this affiliation could also bring for kids in need across America.

We flew right over Manhattan just forty-five minutes before the attacks began. Since Pam is a New Yorker, she was pointing out all the sights on what was an incredibly bright and clear day. We landed in D.C. and found out shortly thereafter that the first tower at the World Trade Center had been hit. Like everyone else in America, we thought it was just an incredible, tragic accident. We continued driving toward D.C., and then the next tower was hit. We were entering Washington, D.C., as we listened to the events unfold on the radio. A few minutes later, the Pentagon was hit — and we were heading straight for downtown. As we rounded a curve, we saw the smoke, but still couldn't comprehend what was happening literally right before our eyes. Our country was under terrorist attack.

People were streaming out of the federal buildings

all around us, talking on cell phones and heading for their homes. We just sat, shocked, in front of our hotel listening to the radio for two hours in our rental car. As the plane in Pennsylvania went down, air traffic control grounded all aircraft; we listened in shocked silence as the radio announcers struggled for words. Then we came out of our daze long enough to take a close look at an area map. We were only five or six blocks from the major Washington sights and other potential targets. We just sat there, staring at the map as if it might hold some answers.

We were scheduled to fly out to Arkansas the next day to visit its Wal-Mart stores. Of course, all flights were canceled, and we ended up driving our rental car all the way home. As we neared home, the New Jersey Turnpike had just been reopened, so we drove parallel to Manhattan Island and saw the plume of smoke where the twin towers of the World Trade Center had been. I cannot describe our experience in any other way except to say that I have never felt more American or more of a father or husband. I couldn't get home fast enough. The experience and the emotions it called forth were overwhelming.

But what was equally awe-inspiring was our unique opportunity to observe firsthand not only the tragedy of the attacks, but the patriotism and generosity of people all over this country as we traveled extensively through the heartlands of America, beginning just a few weeks after September 11. This was partly our job and partly our statement: no terrorist was going to shut down an American dream. It was as simple as that.

I know that Cindy and the kids worried about me and that Pam's family worried about her, but I also know that they were proud as we did our own small part to bring a bit of joy back into the lives of people we met — and of how we stepped up to set an example that would inspire other folks to get back to living their lives.

I had never before traveled extensively in our country's South or Midwest regions. For the rest of that fall, 2001, we traveled to small towns across America, visiting their Wal-Mart Supercenters so I could make "retailtainment" appearances. In the process, we met some of the most amazing people we have ever encountered.

The Pie King ruled! And much like the New England grocers who had inspired and honored me with stories of how Frank Purdue had also tirelessly traveled to stores, Wal-Mart associates told me the stories of Sam Walton's store visits. To be compared in the same sentence with either of these business icons was and remains a huge honor, one that I will carry with me to any project I take on in the future.

Numerous small-town papers carried the story of the little guy (all 6 feet, 9 inches) who grabbed the brass ring and landed his product in Wal-Mart. Then, on January 31, 2002, it was official. I signed documents that finalized my sale of the Gordon's Pie brand to Mrs. Smith's. It was an unbelievable day and one long in the making. I truly believe the realization of my dream could only happen in this country. God bless America.

If you believe it, you can achieve it. Look closely at my story and you will see this undeniable truth. With Infinite Persistence, your wildest dreams can become your reality.

# So Now What?

Since developing — and becoming — the wildly costumed character, King Gordon of Pie, in order to promote Gordon's Pies, I have been able to reach people in ways even *I* never could have imagined. I've always believed that little kids as well as senior citizens are drawn to my character because the Gordon's brand has always been about having fun in a wholesome, old-fashioned way. How, I wondered one day as I noticed their rapt attention, could I capitalize on all this attention in a way that would really help kids?

The answer came from my mom, Dr. Susan Weinberger, who is known throughout the country, and indeed the world, as Dr. Mentor. My mom has been an educator her whole life. When I was growing up, she was a high school Spanish teacher. (To this day, I can fluently say, "Mi madre era una profesora de español por muchos años.") While my sister, Lisa, and I were in high school, my mom went back to school to get her Ph.D.

With that important credential under her belt, she then became the first person in the country to start a school-based mentoring program, located in Norwalk, Connecticut. Today, she has her own business, the Mentor Consulting Group, and she is on the executive board of the National Mentoring Partnership. She travels the world educating businesses and organizations about the benefits of mentoring and instructs them on how to set up their own mentoring programs. She is quite an amazing lady, my mom.

## What, Exactly, Is Mentoring, You Ask?

Mentoring is a concept that has been the subject of quite a lot of discussion lately among those tuned in to serving social causes. Mentoring is the pairing of a caring, responsible adult role model with a child in need in their community. As of this writing, there are approximately 17 million American children on waiting lists for mentors. These kids could be part of programs at local levels, like Boys & Girls Clubs, YMCAs, Big Brothers/Big Sisters, or numerous other school, business, and faith-based programs. And the statistics for kids who are mentored are incredible. The presence of a positive adult role model in their lives at these crucial times means they are statistically much less likely to drop out of school, get involved with drugs, or become teenage parents.

So in late 1999, my mom approached me with a fantastic idea. What if Gordon's Pies became the first food company in America to actively promote mentoring and the National Mentoring Partnership on its packaging? The National Mentoring Partnership (NMP) is the Washington D.C.-based umbrella organization that acts as a clearinghouse for information on mentoring organizations around the country. (Log on to www.mentoring.org or call 888-432-MENTOR to learn about organizations in your area that match kids with positive adult role models.)

Despite the amazing work done by mentoring organizations around the country, the missing ingredient, according to my mom — and the NMP — was public awareness of the profound need for mentors. The idea resonated with me immediately. I was anxious to give back and share the fruits of my success with a worthy cause, and this sounded perfect. We decided that my strength — my talent for promotion and getting attention — was tailor-made for generating increased awareness of this critical need as I traveled across the country in the Piebus. And what better place to reach virtually every American than through its supermarkets? After all, just about everybody shops for food — and even if they don't do the shopping, they still eat!

I immediately redesigned my Gordon's pie box to include an entire side panel devoted to mentoring and to the NMP's Web site. Then I redesigned the Piebus, Piejeep and Pievan to all include "BE A MENTOR," with the NMP's Web site to further promote this wonderful cause.

I began thinking of ways in which I could use my developing celebrity status to personally champion the need for mentors during all of my personal appearances. Then, when Wal-Mart started to nationally distribute Gordon's Pies, my mentoring awareness program got a serious boost. Now millions of Americans are exposed to my message, "Everyone Needs a Mentor, I Still Do," along with the NMP's Web site. In addition, whenever I made personal appearances at Wal-Mart Supercenters across America, with Wal-Mart's permission, I invited the store's local mentoring organizations to join me. These organizations' members would then station themselves outside the front door of the local Supercenter during my appearance and educate customers entering the store about the mentoring opportunities that existed in their communities. In this way, countless folks from Augusta, Maine, to Lincoln, Nebraska, to Salt Lake City, Utah, have learned about the need for mentors in their communities. Like so many nonprofit organizations, local mentoring organizations often don't have the opportunity to get in front of hundreds — much less thousands — of people at a time. It is a feeling of satisfaction I cannot describe to know that my Gordon's Pie Party and Mentor Recruitment Events have successfully raised awareness of the critical need for mentors across the country.

# Pay It Forward

It doesn't matter which cause you choose — the important thing is to pay your successes forward to help others in some way for an even deeper reward. In fact, I have learned that giving back is just as important, if not more so, than succeeding in the first place. Look around and see what human needs most catch your attention. Something, or several things, will surface if you ask for that opportunity. Now look within yourself and decide which cause is most important to you. Then decide how you can best contribute to that cause. It may be time, it may be money, it may be talents or skills, or it may be some combination. But you can be sure that whatever you give will come right back to you in the goodwill you put out in the world.

I know that few people have the opportunity to use a platform like my Gordon's pie box to promote their cause. However, if recycling is your passion, help set up a program in your office or workout club or town. Or if environmental issues are your focus, then start attending your town's planning sessions to find out how land development looks in your community. Volunteer at your local soup kitchen or homeless shelter, if helping one of these causes is your passion. Opportunities exist and needs are everywhere. Just look for them; we all have something to contribute. And whether it is organizing a faith-based event or project, or taking on a cause of national scope, it is our responsibility to figure out what those things are and then to use the skills that created your success to help others. We have so many opportunities to help create positive change. Please don't let the daily pressures of your life stand in the way of making a difference in your world. Share a piece of your dream.

# Living the Full Circle

In life, in love, in business, and in service to others, everything we share and everything we seek to achieve becomes part of our own, individual "full circle." That, I believe, is the fundamental law of the Universe — and it is reflected in the power of pi. If we apply the power of this timeless equation, known as pi, to our desire for success, we can believe, without fear, that we can go as far as we need to go, for as long as necessary, to reach a potential we can't even imagine. By following our hearts, achieving our dreams, and sharing with others, we can accomplish more than we ever imagined. And this infinite result, created by our Infinite Persistence, will not only affect our lives, but the entire world.

## Take a Lesson From Yourself

My experiences in running my company have been life-changing. I have had more than my share of failures, but I feel blessed to have enjoyed extreme success as well. My advice to you is this: learn from yourself, because you really are your own best teacher. Create and strengthen your awareness of these lessons by taking time regularly to reflect on your journey — the experiences, the challenges, and the mistakes. Catalog these learning experiences in your mind so that you will have a reference for future decisions. The challenges will still come, but because of the resource you have created within yourself, the solutions will be easier.

## Enjoy the Pie!

And while you're learning and pursuing your dream, always remember to enjoy the entirety of your journey. Live in the present, and express your appreciation out loud for all the experiences that come your way. See the little things every day that bring you happiness, and make a conscious effort to appreciate them — the little things add up fast. Achieving your dreams is not just about the big successes; it's also about the joys of small triumphs. Don't miss them.

Be grateful for the people in your life. Begin and end each day in a place of gratitude, and the joy of appreciating the people in your life will stay with you. Keep in mind how much the special people in your life care about you and believe in you. Be grateful for their support and encouragement, and always make time for them — no matter how much you have to do or how busy you are.

And finally, remember the history of your life so you do not repeat anything but the positive. Never lose touch with where you started, how you grew up, and how you felt when you became of age. Remember when your journey toward your dream first began, and how far you've come since last year, last month, last week, or yesterday. You can only learn from these experiences if you remember them clearly.

## With Awareness Comes Mastery

It all comes down to awareness, whether it is the awareness of your financial condition or the state of your marriage. I have tried to provide for you some insights into the lessons I learned in my business and my life to help you find new ways to improve your life, perhaps shift your perspective a little, and, ultimately, achieve *your* dream. But more than that, I hope you will take your own lessons to heart when you reach *your* moment of triumph. Imagine the day when you will feel as I did in that conference room high above Atlanta, where I signed the documents that completed the circle of my pie adventure. How will you discover how to share *your* success story and its unique insights?

Remember, it's all about the people you touch in your life. And when you do find a way to touch other's lives in a positive and meaningful way — to help them find their own circle of infinite potential — you will *then* be truly successful far beyond the financial and personal gain of any business endeavor. You will have made a difference in the world. And that is the ultimate level of success in any endeavor.

# Photos

Gordon's family

It all started in a small apple-orchard town in New Hampshire. Gordon Weinberger began making apple pies in his home kitchen.

Gordon Weinberger's home outside New York City.

*Mentoring with
Tom Cruise*

*Gordon with Lee Scott, CEO of
Wal-Mart Stores, Inc.*

# About Gordon Weinberger

At age 28, Gordon Weinberger — an unforgettable, larger-than-life figure almost 7 feet tall, weighing 255 pounds — started Gordon's Pies in a sleepy little New Hampshire town. By the time he was 33, he was a self-made millionaire and had transformed his pie business from a roadside operation to a national multimillion-dollar corporation.

But that doesn't mean things were always this easy for Weinberger. When his pie company teetered on the edge of bankruptcy within the first three years of operation, and with almost $400,000 in outstanding invoices, Weinberger's real story began. By marshaling his strengths — a unique mix of moxie and marketing — Weinberger turned himself into an attention-getting marketing machine that won the notice of news media and talk show hosts nationwide. And by increasing his sales well over $1 million, he was able to snatch his company from the jaws of insurmountable debt.

In 1999, the United States Chamber of Commerce honored Gordon Weinberger with the coveted Blue Chip Enterprise Award. "CNN News" named him "An American Trendsetter." And, as a featured guest on QVC, Weinberger won The Quest for America's Best Tour by selling thousands of Gordon's Apple Pies nationwide in less than three minutes.

For more than half of his career, Gordon Weinberger has been the national spokesman for the National Mentoring Partnership, using his pie boxes to advertise the need for almost 17 million mentors for children on wait-lists across America.

A high-level professional in asset management, public and customer relations, communication, organization, and prioritization, Weinberger has served as consultant to some of the largest companies in the world, including Wal-Mart, Ahold and Sainsbury, to name a few. He also delivers keynote speeches to both private and corporate audiences.

Today Weinberger is the mastermind and creator of the Infinite Persistence™ Life Brand, a concept born of his experiences and his profound understanding of the power of "never giving up, no matter what." By focusing on a few simple, yet powerful, laws of the Universe, Weinberger conveys to today's entrepreneur an unstoppable mentality he calls "Real-Life Marketing" — and how every person can learn to tap into his or her own well of infinite possibilities.

*Gordon Weinberger*